Contents

Easter brownie bites

Prep:15 mins **Cook:**15 mins

Makes 24 mini brownies

Ingredients

- 175g butter , chopped
- 150g dark chocolate
- 250g light brown soft sugar
- 85g self-raising flour
- 50g cocoa powder
- 3 large eggs , beaten
- 100g milk chocolate chips
- 24 mini chocolate eggs , plus extra to decorate

Method

STEP 1

Heat oven to 180C/160C fan/gas 4. Line 24 holes of a mini muffin tray with paper cases. Put the butter, dark chocolate and sugar in a pan and heat it very gently, stirring all the time until the butter and chocolate have melted. Remove from the heat and leave to cool for a few mins.

STEP 2

Meanwhile, sift the flour, cocoa and a good pinch of salt into a large bowl. Stir in the warm, melted chocolate mixture and the beaten eggs, then add half the chocolate chips and mix until just combined.

STEP 3

Divide the mixture between the cases and place a mini egg into the middle of each muffin, pushing down gently. Bake for 12-15 mins until cooked but still gooey in the centre – they will continue cooking a little as they cool down. Leave to cool for 10 mins in the tin before transferring to a wire rack to cool completely.

STEP 4

Melt the rest of the chocolate chips in short bursts in the microwave, or in a bowl set over a pan of simmering water, stirring frequently. Leave to cool until it is quite thick, then dot a small amount on each cake and stick on some more mini eggs.

Salmon pesto traybake with baby roast potatoes

Prep:5 mins **Cook:**45 mins

Serves 2 adults + 2 children

Ingredients

- 500g baby new potatoes, cut in half
- 1 tsp olive oil
- 2 large courgettes, cut into small chunks
- 1 red pepper, cut into small chunks
- 1 spring onion, finely sliced
- 25g pine nuts
- 3-4 salmon fillets
- juice ½ lemon
- 1½ - 2 tbsp pesto

Method

STEP 1

Boil the potatoes for 10 mins until tender, then drain. Heat oven to 200C/180C fan/gas 6. Toss the potatoes in the oil, then transfer to a baking tray. Roast for 20 mins. Push the potatoes to one side and put the courgette, pepper, spring onion and pine nuts down the middle of the tray. Put the salmon on the other side. Squeeze lemon juice over the fillets and the vegetables (not including the potatoes). Season everything with pepper. Spread each of the salmon fillets with pesto and return the tray to the oven for 12-15 mins until everything is cooked through.

Snowy chocolate crackle biscuits

Prep:30 mins **Cook:**45 mins

plus 1 hour chilling

Makes 45-50

Ingredients

- 200g dark chocolate , chopped
- 125g unsalted butter , softened
- 300g soft light brown sugar
- 2 eggs
- 150g plain flour
- 60g cocoa powder
- 2 tsp baking powder
- 2-3 tbsp milk
- 100g icing sugar

Method

STEP 1

Melt the chocolate in a bowl set over a pan of barely simmering water (make sure the base doesn't touch the water), or in a microwave in short bursts. Set aside to cool.

STEP 2

Beat the butter and sugar using electric beaters, then beat in the eggs, flour, cocoa powder, baking powder and chocolate. Pour in the milk to make a soft dough, but don't overmix it. Cover and chill for 1 hr.

STEP 3

Heat oven to 180C/160C fan/gas 4. Line one or two baking sheets with parchment. Put the icing sugar in a bowl. Scoop heaped tablespoons of dough and roll each ball in your hands before dropping it into the icing sugar and rolling it around. Put on baking sheets and repeat, spacing the balls apart.

STEP 4

Bake for about 12-15 mins until the biscuits feel firm when touched. The biscuits should puff up and cracks should open up, too. Leave to cool on the trays, then transfer to wire racks to cool completely. *Will keep for up to a week in an airtight container.*

3-veg mac 'n' cheese

Prep:10 mins **Cook:**40 mins

Serves 2 adults + 2 children

Ingredients

- 150g butternut squash, cut into chunks
- 300g penne (we used Napolina 50% white 50% wholemeal)
- 40g butter
- 1 small leek, finely sliced (about 50g)
- 25g flour
- 600ml milk
- 100g frozen peas
- 175g mature Cheddar cheese (we used a vegetarian version)
- 1 slice day-old brown bread, blitzed into crumbs

Method

STEP 1

Heat oven to 200C/fan 180C/gas 6. Put the butternut squash in a steamer over boiling water. Steam for around 15-20 mins or until tender. Drain and then blitz in a food processor until smooth.

STEP 2

Cook the pasta according to the pack instructions.

STEP 3

Heat the butter in a medium saucepan, add the leek and cook for 2 mins. Stir in the flour and cook for 1-2 mins more. Take the pan off the heat and gradually whisk in the milk. Return to the heat and bring to the boil, stirring all the time. Simmer for 5 mins. Stir in the peas and bring back to a simmer. Take the pan off the heat and stir in the butternut squash, then 125g cheese.

STEP 4

Stir the pasta into the sauce and transfer to an ovenproof dish. Sprinkle over the remaining cheese and the breadcrumbs. Bake for 20 mins or until golden and bubbling.

Gingerbread men

Prep:30 mins **Cook:**10 mins

Serves 15-20

Ingredients

- 225g plain flour , plus extra for dusting
- ½ tsp salt
- 2 tsp bicarbonate of soda
- 1 heaped tsp ground ginger
- ½ tsp cinnamon
- 50g unsalted butter
- 100g soft brown sugar
- 100g golden syrup

Method

STEP 1

Heat oven to 190C/170C fan/gas 5 and line a baking tray with baking parchment. Sieve the flour, salt, bicarb, ginger and cinnamon into a large bowl. Heat the butter, sugar and syrup until dissolved. Leave the sugar mixture to cool slightly, then mix into the dry ingredients to form a dough. Chill the dough in the fridge for 30 mins.

STEP 2

On a surface lightly dusted with flour, roll out the dough to a ¼-inch thickness. Stamp out the gingerbread men shapes with a cutter, then re-roll any off-cuts and repeat. Place your gingerbread shapes on the lined trays, allowing space for them to spread. Cook for 10-15 mins, then remove from the oven and leave to cool.

Snowman cake

Prep:1 hr **Cook:**30 mins

Serves 16

Ingredients

- 225g unsalted butter , softened, plus extra for the tin
- 225g golden caster sugar

- 4 large eggs
- ½ lemon , zested
- 1 tsp vanilla extract
- 225g self-raising flour
- splash of milk

For the buttercream

- 125g unsalted butter , softened
- 300g icing sugar , sieved
- ½ tsp vanilla extract
- 1 tbsp milk

To decorate

- icing sugar , for dusting
- 500g pack white fondant icing
- ready-to-roll icing (we used a mixed pack green, blue, orange and black, or you can use white fondant icing mixed with food colouring)

Method

STEP 1

Heat oven to 180C/160C fan/gas 4. Butter and line the bases of two 18-19cm cake tins with baking parchment.

STEP 2

Beat the butter and sugar with an electric whisk until pale and fluffy. Add the eggs, one at a time, and beat well, scraping down the sides of the bowl after each addition. Add the lemon zest, vanilla, flour, milk and a pinch of salt and blend until just combined, then evenly divide the mixture between the tins.

STEP 3

Bake in the centre of the oven for 25-30 mins until a skewer inserted into the middle of each cake comes out clean. Cool the cakes in their tins for 10 mins, then turn out onto a wire rack and leave to cool completely.

STEP 4

To make the buttercream, put the butter in a large bowl and beat with an electric whisk until fluffy. Add the icing sugar 2-3 tbsp at a time until it is all incorporated, adding the vanilla and milk halfway through. Sandwich the cakes together with a little of the buttercream and put on a board. Use the remaining buttercream to cover the sides and top of the cake. Chill for 30 mins.

STEP 5

To decorate, roll out the white fondant icing on a surface lightly dusted with icing sugar until large enough to cover the top and sides of the cake. Drape the fondant icing over the cake and carefully mould to fit. Trim off any excess, wrap and set aside.

STEP 6

Roll out the green icing and cut out a semi-circle, using the base of the cake tin as a guide; this will be the snowman's hat. Brush one side with a little water and stick on the cake. Cut a strip of green icing and make some markings to make it look like the band of a hat, then trim to the correct length and stick on.

STEP 7

To make the nose, shape a round, flat lump from the orange icing. Mark a smile by gently pressing the rim of a water glass into the fondant. Cut out two circles from the black icing for the eyes, then add a small circle of white icing (from the offcuts) to make the eyes appear to sparkle. To make the scarf, wrap a strip of the blue icing around the base of the cake, then use a knife to add cuts for the fringe. Will keep for up to a week in an airtight container in a cool place.

Broccoli pasta shells

Prep:5 mins **Cook:**15 mins

Serves 4

Ingredients

- 1 head of broccoli, chopped into florets
- 1 garlic clove, unpeeled
- 2 tbsp olive oil
- 250g pasta shells
- ½ small pack parsley
- ½ small pack basil
- 30g toasted pine nuts
- ½ lemon, zested and juiced
- 30g parmesan (or vegetarian alternative), plus extra to serve

Method

STEP 1

Heat the oven to 200C/180C fan/gas 6. Toss the broccoli and garlic in 1 tbsp of the olive oil on a roasting tray and roast in the oven for 10-12 mins, until softened.

STEP 2

Tip the pasta shells into a pan of boiling, salted water. Cook according to packet instructions and drain. Tip the parsley, basil, pine nuts, lemon juice and parmesan into a blender. Once the broccoli is done, set aside a few of the smaller pieces. Squeeze the garlic from its skin, add to the blender along with the rest of the broccoli, pulse to a pesto and season well.

STEP 3

Toss the pasta with the pesto. Add the reserved broccoli florets, split between two bowls and top with a little extra parmesan, the lemon zest and a good grinding of black pepper, if you like.

Easiest ever biscuits

Prep:10 mins **Cook:**20 mins

makes 24

Ingredients

- 200g unsalted butter, softened
- 200g golden caster sugar
- 1 large egg
- ½ tsp vanilla extract
- 400g plain flour, plus extra for dusting

Method

STEP 1

Heat the oven to 200C/180C fan/gas 6 and line a baking sheet with baking parchment. Put the butter in a bowl and beat it with electric beaters until soft and creamy. Beat in the sugar, then the egg and vanilla, and finally the flour to make a dough. If the dough feels a bit sticky, add a little bit more flour and knead it in.

STEP 2

Pull pieces off the dough and roll them out to about the thickness of two £1 coins on a floured surface. The easiest way to do this with small children is to roll the mixture out on a baking mat. Cut out shapes using a 9cm biscuit cutter, or a use the rim of a small glass and peel away the leftover dough around the edges. Press some clean toys gently into the biscuits, making sure you make enough of a mark without going all the way through. Re-roll off-cuts and repeat.

STEP 3

Transfer the whole mat or the individual biscuits to the baking sheet and bake for 8-10 mins or until the edges are just brown. Leave to cool for 5 mins, then serve. *Will keep for three days in a biscuit tin.*

Candy apples

Prep:20 mins **Cook:**15 mins

Serves 8

Ingredients

- 8 red apples
- 400g caster sugar
- 1 tsp lemon juice
- 4 tbsp golden syrup
- a few drops red food colouring (optional)

You will also need

- 8 sticks , chopsticks or lolly sticks

Method

STEP 1

Remove the stalks from the apples, then put them in a heatproof bowl and pour over boiling water from the kettle to cover them and leave for 3-4 mins. Remove with a slotted spoon and pat dry. (This removes the protective wax from the skin and makes the toffee stick to the apples better.)

STEP 2

Push the sharpest end of each stick into the stalk-end of each apple, making sure it's firmly wedged in. Put a large piece of baking parchment on a board.

STEP 3

Tip the sugar into a large saucepan, add the lemon juice and 100ml water. Bring to a simmer and cook until the sugar has dissolved. Swirl the pan gently to move the sugar around, but don't stir. Add the golden syrup and simmer the mixture (be careful it doesn't boil over) until it reaches 'hard crack' stage or 150C on a sugar thermometer. If you don't have a thermometer, test the toffee by dropping a small amount into cold water. It should harden instantly and, when removed, be brittle. If it's soft, continue to boil. When it's ready, drip in some food colouring, if you like, and swirl to combine. Turn off the heat.

STEP 4

Working quickly, dip each apple into the toffee, tipping the pan to cover it fully. Lift out and allow any excess to drip off back into the pan before placing on the baking parchment. Repeat with the remaining apples. Gently heat the toffee again, if you need to. Leave to set. *Best eaten on the same day.*

Green burgers

Prep:30 mins **Cook:**20 mins

makes 8 (4 for now, 4 for the freezer)

Ingredients

- 2 tbsp olive oil
- 2 onions , finely chopped
- 250g bag spinach
- 5 slices white bread , blitzed into breadcrumbs (or 150g dried breadcrumbs)
- good grating of fresh nutmeg
- 100g mature cheddar , grated
- 40g parmesan , finely grated
- 1-2 large eggs , beaten
- 3 tbsp plain flour

To serve

- 6 crusty bread rolls
- 4 ripe, juicy tomatoes , thickly sliced
- good-quality ketchup or other relish
- sweet potato fries (optional)

Method

STEP 1

Heat half the oil in a frying pan and gently fry the onions for about 10 mins until pale and soft, then leave to cool a little.

STEP 2

Finely chop the spinach in a food processor and tip into a bowl. Add the cooled onion, breadcrumbs, nutmeg, cheddar and Parmesan, and mash together. Add the beaten egg, a little at a time (you may not need all of it), until the mixture holds together. Divide into eight (see tip below) and shape into fat burgers.

STEP 3

Put the flour in a shallow bowl, season well and dip the burgers into the flour to coat. Store in a plastic container between layers of baking parchment. Either chill until ready to cook, or freeze.

STEP 4

Heat the remaining oil in the frying pan and fry for about 5 mins each side until browned all over. Serve in the crusty rolls, with a couple of slices of tomato, ketchup and sweet potato fries on the side, if you like.

Chocolate orange fudge crinkle biscuits

Prep:20 mins **Cook:**10 mins

plus 1 hr chilling (optional)

Makes 35-40 mini biscuits

Ingredients

- 60g cocoa powder , sieved
- 230g caster sugar
- 60ml vegetable oil
- 2 large oranges , zested
- 2 large eggs
- 180g plain flour
- 1 tsp baking powder
- few drops of orange food colouring , or use red and yellow
- 40g icing sugar

Method

STEP 1

Mix the cocoa, 200g caster sugar and oil together with most of the orange zest. Whisk in the eggs one at a time, until fully combined.

STEP 2

Stir the flour, baking powder and a pinch of salt together in a separate bowl, then add to the cocoa mixture and mix until you form a soft dough. If the dough feels very soft, transfer it to the fridge and chill for 1 hr.

STEP 3

Heat the oven to 190C/170C fan/gas 5 and line a baking tray with baking parchment. Tip the remaining caster sugar into a small bowl. Add a drop of food colouring and stir it through the sugar until it's all coloured – add more if you want a stronger colour. Stir in the icing sugar until all of the sugar is coloured, then stir in the remaining orange zest.

STEP 4

Form a heaped teaspoon of the dough into a ball, then roll in the sugar to coat, you might have to press the sugar on, particularly if you've chilled the dough. If the sugar is not sticking well, roll the balls of dough between your hands until the mixture warms up a little. Repeat with the remaining dough, then put, evenly spaced, on the baking tray.

STEP 5

Bake in the centre of the oven for 10 mins – they will crinkle as they cook. The biscuits will firm up as they cool so don't overcook them. Transfer to a wire rack and leave to cool. *Will keep for four days in a biscuit tin.*

Flatbreads with brunch-style eggs

Prep:20 mins **Cook:**15 mins

plus 30 mins proving

Serves 6

Ingredients

- 110g self-raising flour , plus extra for dusting
- 110g atta or plain wholemeal flour
- 3 tbsp rapeseed oil , plus extra for the bowl and frying
- small knob of butter , melted

For the eggs

- 1 tbsp olive oil
- 12 cherry tomatoes , halved
- 4 large eggs
- 25g grated cheddar
- 2 tbsp double cream

Method

STEP 1

Sift the flours and 1 tsp salt into a large bowl. Add 1 tbsp of the oil and 150ml warm water. Bring together into a soft but not too sticky dough (you may need up to 175ml water). If it feels too wet, add some flour. If it's too dry, add water.

STEP 2

Tip onto a floured surface and knead for 4-5 mins, or until smooth. Put the dough in an oiled bowl, cover and leave for 30 mins.

STEP 3

Tip onto a floured surface. Divide into six balls and roll each out into a thin, 18-20cm wide circle using a rolling pin. If you prefer, you can divide again into twelve balls to make smaller flatbreads.

STEP 4

Brush a heavy-based pan with oil and cook one flatbread over a high heat for 1-2 mins on each side, or until golden and starting to puff. Put on a plate and brush with butter. Repeat with the rest of the dough.

STEP 5

Meanwhile, for the eggs, heat the oil in a small non-stick pan and cook the tomatoes briefly until just softened. Season. Crack the eggs into the pan, add the cheese and cream, cover and cook for 2 mins. Remove the lid. Cook until the egg whites are set, then serve from the pan with the flatbreads, making sure the pan has cooled a little first.

Frozen banana lollies

Prep:10 mins **Cook:**5 mins

Serves 4

Ingredients

- 2 bananas
- 4 large strawberries
- 100g natural yogurt
- 200g dark chocolate
- 1 tbsp hundreds and thousands

You will also need:

- 4 wooden lolly sticks

Method

STEP 1

Peel the bananas and trim off the very ends if you'd like them neater. Then chop them each into 4 equal-sized chunks. Thread a strawberry onto each lolly stick first, then push on the pieces of banana.

STEP 2

When all your banana pops are made lay them on a baking tray and put in the freezer, uncovered, for 1 hr.

STEP 3

Put the yogurt into a tall glass or jug then dip each banana pop into the yogurt to coat (avoiding the strawberries), then place back onto the tray to refreeze until set.

STEP 4

Melt the chocolate in the microwave in 30 second bursts (stirring after each blast) then pour into a mug. Dip the end piece of each banana pop in the chocolate then sprinkle over the hundreds and thousands.

STEP 5

The chocolate should set pretty much instantaneously, but you can keep them in the freezer until you want to serve them for up to 1 week.

Vegan Thai green curry

Prep:10 mins **Cook:**20 mins

Serves 4

Ingredients

- 200g baby potatoes, halved
- 100g green beans, trimmed and halved
- 1 tbsp rapeseed oil
- 1 garlic clove, finely sliced
- 1 tbsp Thai green curry paste (check the label to make sure it's vegetarian/ vegan)
- 400g can light coconut milk
- 1 lime, zest pared in thick strips
- 80g sugar snap peas, halved lengthways
- 150g cherry tomatoes, halved
- 100g firm tofu, chopped into small cubes
- small bunch coriander, chopped
- 200g jasmine rice, cooked following pack instructions

Method

STEP 1

Cook the potatoes in boiling water for 8 mins. Add the green beans and cook for a further 3 mins, then drain.

STEP 2

Heat the oil in a wok or pan, fry the garlic for 1 min, add the curry paste and cook for 1 min, or until it starts to darken a little and smell fragrant. Stir in the coconut milk and bring to a simmer, drop in the lime zest and gently bubble for 5 mins to thicken the sauce a little.

STEP 3

Add the potatoes and beans followed by the sugar snap peas and cook for 1 min before stirring in the cherry tomatoes and tofu.

STEP 4

Cut the lime in half and squeeze the juice into the pan, then stir in the coriander and serve over the rice.

Three-minute blender banana pancakes

Prep:1 min **Cook:**2 mins

Serves 2

Ingredients

- small knob of butter , for frying
- 1 banana
- 1 egg
- 1 heaped tbsp self-raising flour
- ½ tsp baking powder
- chopped strawberries and banana, to serve (optional)
- maple syrup , to serve (optional)

Method

STEP 1

Melt the butter in a non-stick frying pan over a low-medium heat. Meanwhile, add the banana, egg, flour and baking powder to a blender and blitz for 20 seconds.

STEP 2

Pour three little puddles straight from the blender into the frying pan. Cook for 1 min or until the tops start to bubble, then flip with a fork or a fish slice and cook for 20-30 seconds more. Repeat with the rest of the mixture to make three more pancakes.

STEP 3

Serve the pancakes with chopped strawberries or banana and a splash of maple syrup, if you like.

Chocolate Rice Krispie cakes

Prep:15 mins **Cook:**5 mins

Makes 9

Ingredients

- 100g milk chocolate, broken up
- 50g dark chocolate, broken up
- 100g butter
- 4 tbsp golden syrup
- 100g rice pops (we used Rice Krispies)

To decorate

- 50g milk chocolate, melted
- sprinkles, mini marshmallows, nuts, Smarties, dried fruit or white chocolate buttons

Method

STEP 1

Put the chocolate in a heatproof bowl with the butter and golden syrup and gently melt in 10-second bursts in the microwave, or melt it over a pan of simmering water, making sure the bowl doesn't touch the water. Stir until smooth, then take off the heat and stir in the rice pops, coating them gently with the chocolate until they are all completely covered.

STEP 2

Divide the mixture between nine cupcake or 12 fairy cake paper cases – it's easier if you slide these into a muffin tin as it will help them hold their shape. Leave to set. If you want them to set faster, put in the fridge for 1 hr.

STEP 3

Drizzle with a little melted chocolate and decorate with sweets, dried fruit or nuts while they are still wet enough to stick them on. Will keep in an airtight container for five days.

Gingerbread people

Prep:45 mins **Cook:**12 mins - 15 mins

Plus chilling, cooling and at least 1 hr drying

Serves 15 - 20

Ingredients

- 175g dark muscovado sugar
- 85g golden syrup
- 100g butter
- 350g plain flour, plus extra for dusting
- 1 tsp bicarbonate of soda
- 1 tbsp ground ginger
- 1 tsp ground cinnamon
- 1 egg, beaten

To decorate

- ready-made writing icing
- chocolate buttons or small sweets (optional)

Method

STEP 1

Melt the sugar, golden syrup and butter in a saucepan, then bubble for 1-2 mins. Leave to cool for about 10 mins.

STEP 2

Tip the flour, bicarbonate of soda and spices into a large bowl. Add the warm syrup mixture and the egg, stir everything together, then gently knead in the bowl until smooth and streak-free. The dough will firm up once cooled. Wrap in cling film and chill for at least 30 mins.

STEP 3

Remove the dough from the fridge, leave at room temperature until softened. Heat the oven to 200C/180C fan/gas 6 and line two baking trays with baking parchment.

STEP 4

Roll out the dough to the thickness of a £1 coin, then cut out gingerbread people with a cutter. Re-roll the excess dough and keep cutting until it's all used up.

STEP 5

Lift the biscuits onto the trays and bake for 10-12 mins, swapping the trays over halfway through cooking. Leave to cool on the trays for 5 mins, then transfer to a wire rack to cool completely. Use the icing to decorate the biscuits as you wish, and stick on chocolate or sweets for buttons. Leave to dry for 1-2 hrs. *Will keep for up to three days in an airtight container.*

Sticky pork lettuce wraps

Prep:20 mins **Cook:**10 mins

Serves 4

Ingredients

- 2 tbsp soy sauce
- 2 tbsp honey
- 2 tbsp brown sugar
- pinch cinnamon
- pinch five-spice powder
- 4 thin-cut pork loin steaks
- 1 carrot , sliced into matchsticks
- 1 lime , juiced
- pinch golden caster sugar
- 1 tbsp rapeseed oil
- ½ cucumber , cut into matchsticks
- 16 soft lettuce leaves (we used Butterhead lettuce)
- sweet chilli sauce , to serve

Method

STEP 1

Make the marinade by mixing the soy with the honey, brown sugar, spices and 1 tbsp water. Put the pork in a shallow bowl, pour the marinade over, turning to make sure the steaks are well coated, then leave to marinate for at least 30 mins.

STEP 2

Mix the carrot with the lime juice and caster sugar. Brush a piece of foil with oil and line the grill pan. Grill the pork steaks (or griddle if you prefer) for 4 mins each side. Keep an eye on them in case the sugar in the marinade starts to blacken. When cooked, cut the pork into strips.

STEP 3

Put the lettuce leaves out on a board and divide the pork between them. Add some carrot and cucumber, then fold in both ends of the lettuce leaf and roll up from one side to contain the filling. Serve with sweet chilli sauce, if you like.

Salmon egg-fried rice

Prep:10 mins **Cook:**10 mins

Serves 2 - 3

Ingredients

- thumb-sized piece ginger, grated
- 1-2 garlic cloves, grated
- 2 tbsp low-salt soy sauce
- ½ tbsp rice wine or sherry vinegar
- 2 tbsp vegetable oil
- 1 large carrot, chopped into chunks
- 175g pack baby corn & mangetout or sugar snap peas, chopped
- 2 skinless salmon fillets
- 250g pouch cooked brown basmati rice
- 2 eggs
- hot sauce, to serve

Method

STEP 1

Mix the ginger, garlic, soy and vinegar, and set aside. Heat a large pan or wok and add 1 tbsp oil, the vegetables and salmon. Fry the salmon for 2 mins each side until it begins to turn opaque. Tip in the rice and stir, flaking the fish into large pieces, then move everything to the side of the pan.

STEP 2

Add the remaining oil to the pan, crack in the eggs and stir to roughly scramble them. Once cooked, stir through the rice and pour over the soy marinade. Season and leave to bubble away for a few mins more, so that all the rice is coated in the sauce. Serve in bowls with hot sauce for drizzling.

One-pan egg & veg brunch

Prep:5 mins **Cook:**25 mins

Serves 2 adults + 2 children

Ingredients

- 300g baby new potatoes , halved
- ½ tbsp rapeseed oil
- 1 knob of butter
- 1 courgette , cut into small chunks
- 1 yellow pepper , cut into small chunks

- 1 red pepper , cut into small chunks
- 2 spring onions , finely sliced
- 1 garlic clove , crushed
- 1 sprig thyme , leaves picked
- 4 eggs
- toast , to serve

Method

STEP 1

Boil the new potatoes for 8 mins, then drain.

STEP 2

Heat the oil and butter in a large non-stick frying pan, then add the courgette, peppers, potatoes and a little salt and pepper. Cook for 10 mins, stirring from time to time until everything is starting to brown. Add the spring onions, garlic and thyme and cook for 2 mins more.

STEP 3

Make four spaces in the pan and crack in the eggs. Cover with foil or a lid and cook for around 4 mins, or until the eggs are cooked (with the yolks soft for dipping into). Sprinkle with more thyme leaves and ground black pepper if you like. Serve with toast.

Christmas truffles

Prep:30 mins **Cook:**5 mins

plus 7 hrs chilling

Makes 35

Ingredients

- 150g dark chocolate, chopped
- 150g milk chocolate, chopped
- 150ml double cream
- 50g unsalted butter
- cocoa powder, sprinkles, lustre powder, icing sugar, chopped nuts, for coating
- flavourless oil (such as sunflower), for shaping

Method

STEP 1

Put the dark and milk chocolate in a bowl, then put the cream and butter in a pan and bring to a simmer. Pour the hot cream over the chocolate and stir until it melts. Leave to cool, then chill in the fridge for 7 hrs.

STEP 2

Put the coatings into separate bowls. To shape the truffles, lightly rub your hands with flavourless oil and roll teaspoons of the truffle mix between your palms – this can get messy!

STEP 3

Gently roll the truffles in the bowl until evenly coated, then put in a box and chill. *Store in the fridge in an airtight container for three days, or freeze for up to a month. Defrost in the fridge overnight.*

Quick banana ice cream sandwiches

Prep:15 mins **Cook:**12 mins

Serves 4

Ingredients

- 200g peanut butter (crunchy or smooth is fine)
- 175g golden caster sugar
- 75g dark chocolate , chopped into chunks
- 1 large egg

For the ice cream

- 3 bananas , peeled, chopped and frozen in advance
- 2 tbsp double cream
- 1 tsp vanilla essence

Method

STEP 1

Heat oven to 180C/fan 160C/gas 4 and line two large baking sheets with baking parchment. Put the peanut butter, sugar, ¼ tsp fine table salt and chocolate chunks in a bowl and mix well with a wooden spoon. Crack in the egg and mix again until the mixture clumps together and forms a dough.

STEP 2

Break off chunks of dough (about the size of a cherry tomato) and arrange them, spaced apart, on the sheets. Press the cookies down with the back of a fork to squash them a little. (The cookies can be frozen for up to two months – to cook from frozen, add an extra 1-2 mins to the cooking time.) Bake for about 12 mins until golden around the edges and paler in the centre. Leave to cool on the trays for 5 mins.

STEP 3

Meanwhile, put the bananas, cream and vanilla in a food processor and blend until they make a thick ice cream. Scoop into balls with an ice cream scoop, and sandwich between the cookies. Serve immediately.

Butternut squash & chickpea tagine

Prep:5 mins **Cook:**25 mins

Serves 2 adults + 2 children

Ingredients

- 1 tbsp oil
- 1 red onion , finely chopped
- 2 garlic cloves , crushed
- 1 tsp grated ginger
- ½ tsp ground cumin
- 1 tsp ground coriander
- 1 tsp cinnamon
- ¼ tsp mild chilli powder
- 500g bag frozen butternut squash chunks
- 2 carrots , cut into small dice
- 1 courgette , cut into small dice
- 2 x 400g cans chopped tomatoes
- 1 x 400g can chickpeas , drained
- cooked couscous or rice, to serve

Method

STEP 1

Heat the oil in a heavy-based pan, then slowly cook the onions for around 10 mins until starting to caramelise. Stir in the garlic, ginger and spices and cook for a further 2 mins. Add the vegetables and canned tomatoes and bring to a simmer. Put the lid on and simmer for around 15 mins or until all the veg are tender. Stir in the chickpeas, heat through and serve with couscous or rice.

Giant cookie

Prep: 15 mins **Cook:** 20 mins

Serves 6 - 8

Ingredients

- 200g butter at room temperature, plus extra for the pan
- 250g light brown sugar
- 2 egg yolks
- ½ tsp vanilla extract
- 275g plain flour
- 1 tsp baking powder
- 150g chocolate chips
- 100g other cookie fillings, such as pretzels, chopped nuts, pieces of fudge or toffee, marshmallows
- vanilla ice cream, to serve (optional)

Method

STEP 1

Heat oven to 180C/160C fan/gas 4. Tip the butter and sugar into a large mixing bowl, beat until combined, then stir in the yolks and vanilla. Tip in the flour, baking powder, chocolate chips, a pinch of sea salt and any other fillings you want to add. Mix until a crumbly dough forms.

STEP 2

Lightly butter a 25cm ovenproof frying pan. Spoon in and flatten the cookie mixture. For a gooey dessert, bake for 20 mins, leave to rest for 5 mins, then scoop straight from the pan and serve with ice cream, if you like. For a firmer cookie you can cut, bake for 30 mins, then leave to cool completely before cutting into wedges.

Pick & mix pesto pasta salad bar

Prep: 10 mins **Cook:** 15 mins

Serves 6

Ingredients

- 400g of your favourite pasta (shells or butterflies work well)
- 3 tbsp olive oil
- 3 tbsp pesto

- 100g frozen peas , defrosted
- 100g sweetcorn from a can, drained (or use defrosted frozen sweetcorn)
- 290g pack baby mozzarella
- 100g cherry tomatoes , halved
- 50g pitted black olives , halved
- 3 spring onions , trimmed and chopped

Method

STEP 1

Cook the pasta following pack instructions, then drain and toss in 1 tbsp oil. Transfer to a large bowl and set aside to cool, tossing occasionally so the pasta doesn't stick. Mix the remaining olive oil with the pesto and set aside. *Both can be prepared up to two days ahead, then covered and chilled.*

STEP 2

Put all the ingredients into individual bowls and serve with a large empty bowl and wooden spoon for mixing individual portions of pasta salad with your choice of ingredients.

Chicken & chickpea rice

Prep:15 mins **Cook:**25 mins

Serves 2-3

Ingredients

- 25g butter
- 1 shallot , finely chopped
- 1 skinless chicken breast (about 180g), cut into strips
- 1 carrot (about 100g), cut into thin batons
- 1 cinnamon stick
- 1 strip lemon zest
- 125g basmati rice
- 2 heaped tbsp raisins or sultanas
- 250ml chicken stock
- 215g can chickpeas (drained weight 130g)

Method

STEP 1

Melt half the butter in a frying pan with a lid. Fry the shallot for a couple of minutes, then add the chicken and carrot. Fry the veg until starting to brown, then add the cinnamon and lemon, and season well. Stir in the rice and raisins, then add the stock and bring to a simmer.

STEP 2

Scatter the chickpeas on top, then cover with the lid. Cook for 15 mins over a low heat until the rice has absorbed all the stock – if the rice is still firm, add 50ml water. Stand for 5 mins, then fluff up the rice. Dot over the remaining butter, then serve.

Simple iced biscuits

Prep:30 mins **Cook:**20 mins

Makes 40-45

Ingredients

- 200g unsalted butter , softened
- 200g golden caster sugar
- 1 large egg
- ½ tsp vanilla extract or 1 lemon, zested
- 400g plain flour , plus extra for dusting

To decorate

- 8-12 x 19g coloured icing pens , or fondant icing sugar mixed with a little water and food colouring

Method

STEP 1

Heat oven to 200C/180C fan/gas 6. Put the butter in a bowl and beat it using an electric whisk until soft and creamy. Beat in the sugar, then the egg and vanilla or lemon, and finally the flour to make a dough. If the dough feels a bit sticky, add a little more flour and knead it in.

STEP 2

Cut the dough into six pieces and roll out one at a time to about 5mm thickness on a floured surface. The easiest way to do this is to roll the mixture out on a baking mat. Cut out letter and number shapes (we used 7 x 4cm cutters) and peel away the leftover dough at the edges. Re-roll any off-cuts and repeat.

STEP 3

Transfer the whole mat or the individual biscuits to two baking sheets (transfer them to baking parchment if not using a mat) and bake for 7-10 mins or until the edges are just brown. Leave to cool completely and repeat with the rest of the dough. You should be able to fit about 12 on each sheet. If you are using two sheets, then the one underneath will take a minute longer.

STEP 4

Ice the biscuits using the pens to make stripes or dots, or colour in the whole biscuit if you like. They will keep for five days in an airtight container.

Child-friendly Thai chicken noodles

Prep:10 mins **Cook:**15 mins - 20 mins

Serves 2 adults + 2 children

Ingredients

- 100g sugar snap peas
- 1 tbsp oil
- 2 spring onions , finely chopped
- 2 garlic cloves , crushed
- 1 tsp grated ginger
- 3 x chicken breasts, cut into chunks
- ½ tbsp Thai curry paste (we used Thai Taste)
- 400ml can coconut milk
- limes , juice of one, other quartered
- 50g frozen peas
- nests egg noodles
- handful chopped coriander , to serve

Method

STEP 1

Blanch the sugar snap peas in a bowl of boiling water for 2 mins, then drain. Heat the oil in a large frying pan. Add the spring onions, garlic, ginger and chicken. Gently fry for 2-3 mins. Stir in the curry paste and cook for 1 minute more. Add the coconut milk to the pan, along with a splash of water, the lime juice, peas and sugar snap peas. Gently bubble for around 5 mins until the chicken is cooked through.

STEP 2

Meanwhile, cook the noodles according to the pack instructions. Drain. Stir the noodles through the sauce, scatter with coriander and serve with a wedge of lime for squeezing over.

Caramel & coffee ice cream sandwich

Prep:5 mins

Serves 2

Ingredients

- 1 tbsp chocolate-coated coffee beans , roughly chopped
- 2 scoops coffee ice cream , softened
- 4 caramel wafers

Method

STEP 1

Mix the chocolate coffee beans into the softened ice cream until combined, then transfer to a small loaf tin and freeze for a few hours or until solid.

STEP 2

Use cookie cutters to cut the ice cream to the same size as the waffles, then sandwich between two waffles.

Creamy salmon, prawn & almond curry

Prep:15 mins **Cook:**25 mins

Serves 3 (or 2 adults and 2 children)

Ingredients

- 2 tbsp oil
- 1 onion , chopped
- 2 garlic cloves , crushed
- 2 red peppers , sliced
- ½ tsp ground turmeric
- 2 tsp ground cumin
- 2 tsp ground coriander
- 1 tbsp tomato purée
- 70g ground almonds
- 1 low-salt vegetable or chicken stock cube
- 1½ tbsp double cream
- 300g green beans
- 2 salmon fillets (around 300g-350g), skin removed and cut into chunks
- 150g raw king prawns
- handful of coriander , leaves picked
- 150g brown rice , cooked, to serve

- ½ lime , cut into wedges to serve

Method

STEP 1

Heat the oil in a pan and cook the onion for 8-10 mins until starting to soften, then stir in the garlic and cook for 1 min. Add the peppers, spices, tomato purée and a splash of water. Cook for 1-2 mins until the peppers soften.

STEP 2

Add the almonds, stock cube and 500ml water to the pan, season and simmer for 10 mins. Stir in the cream. Cook the beans in a small pan of boiling water for 2 mins until just tender, then drain.

STEP 3

When you're ready to eat, add the salmon to the sauce, simmer gently for 2-3 mins until the fish turns opaque, then add the prawns and cook for a further 1 min until they turn pink. Check the salmon is cooked through (it should easily flake when gently pressed with a knife). Remove from the heat and add a little lime juice. Serve scattered with the coriander, the beans with the rice and the lime wedges for squeezing over.

Watermelon doughnuts

Prep:20 mins **Cook:**10 mins

Makes 12 large doughnuts

Ingredients

For the batter

- 200g plain flour
- 180g golden caster sugar
- 2 tsp baking powder
- ½ tsp ground cinnamon
- 250g buttermilk
- 2 medium eggs , lightly beaten
- 30g butter , melted
- 1 tsp vanilla extract

To decorate

- 300g pink candy melts
- 200g green candy melts

- 2 tbsp vegetable oil
- 30g dark chocolate chips

You will need

- 12-hole doughnut tin

Method

STEP 1

Heat oven to 220C/200C fan/gas 7. Put all the dry ingredients together in a bowl and mix well with a whisk to distribute the cinnamon and baking powder. Add the wet ingredients and mix until just combined. Pour the batter into a piping bag and fill the doughnut pan until each hole is approximately three quarters full. Do this in batches if needed.

STEP 2

Bake for 9–10 minutes until risen, golden brown and the tops are springy to the touch. Allow to cool for a couple of mins then turn out onto a wire rack to cool completely. If the doughnuts have lost their holes during baking use a small cutter or piping nozzle to recut them.

STEP 3

Put your pink candy melts in a microwaveable bowl with 1 tbsp vegetable oil. Melt at 30 second intervals at a medium heat until silky and completely melted. Spoon the pink candy melt over the top of each doughnut wiping off any drips that fall down the edge. Leave on a wire rack until set (about 5-10 mins). Do not throw away the excess pink!

STEP 4

Meanwhile melt the green candy melts in the same way. Hold your doughnuts on the edge and roll them through the green candy melts only covering the outside not the pink. Leave to set.

STEP 5

Cut the chocolate chips in half to create watermelon seed shapes. Dip a cocktail stick into the pink candy melt and mark out the spots to place your seeds then stick on the chocolate chips.

Pea & pesto soup with fish finger croûtons

Prep:5 mins **Cook:**15 mins

Serves 4

Ingredients

- 500g frozen pea

- 4 medium potatoes, peeled and cut into cubes
- 1l hot vegetable stock
- 300g pack fish finger (about 10)
- 3 tbsp green pesto

Method

STEP 1

Tip the peas and potatoes into a large saucepan, then pour in the stock. Bring to the boil and simmer for 10 mins, until the potato chunks are tender. Meanwhile, grill the fish fingers as per pack instructions until cooked through and golden. Cut into bitesize cubes and keep warm.

STEP 2

Take a third of the peas and potatoes out of the pan with a slotted spoon and set aside. Blend the rest of the soup until smooth, then stir in the pesto with the reserved vegetables. Heat through and serve in warm bowls with the fish finger croûtons on top.

Cherry ripple, chocolate & rose ice cream

Prep:15 mins

Plus 4 hrs freezing

Serves 8

Ingredients

- 425g can pitted cherries in syrup, drained (reserve the syrup)
- ½ tsp rose water
- 600ml double cream
- ½a 397g can condensed milk
- 100g bar of dark chocolate , chopped (you want a nice mixture of chunks and smaller bits)
- shortbread biscuits , cones and extra cherries, to serve (optional)

Method

STEP 1

Line a 900g loaf tin with parchment or cling film. Tip the cherries into a food processor with 2 tbsp syrup from the tin, add the rose water and blend to a purée.

STEP 2

Whip the cream until it holds soft peaks, then stir in the condensed milk and half the cherry purée. Pour roughly a third of the mixture into the loaf tin, swirl through some of the purée and scatter with chocolate, then repeat the layers until you've used all the ingredients up. Freeze for at least 4 hrs. Turn out the ice cream, slice and serve with biscuits and extra cherries, or use a scoop for balls to fill ice cream cones.

Weaning recipe: Fish pie bites

Prep:20 mins **Cook:**1 hr and 45 mins

Makes 8-9 bites

Ingredients

- 1 medium baking potato
- 1 small salmon fillet , about 120g
- 1 tbsp frozen sweetcorn and peas, defrosted
- 1 tsp fresh chives , snipped into little strands
- 25g mild cheddar , grated
- ½ small egg , beaten
- oil , for greasing

Method

STEP 1

Heat the oven to 200C/ 180 fan/ gas 6. Wrap the potato in foil, place on a baking tray and roast in the oven for 1 hour 15 mins. Wrap the fish in foil, put on the same tray and continue cooking for around 10-12 mins until opaque and cooked through.

STEP 2

Once cooked, halve the potato and scoop out the filling. Flake the fish, removing any bones and discarding the skin.

STEP 3

Grease a baking tray with a little oil. Mash the potato, then mix through the flaked fish, veg, chives, cheese and egg. Allow to cool a little, then take golf-ball sized dollops of mixture and form into little croquette shapes. Arrange on a foil-lined tray and chill in the fridge for 30 mins. *If freezing, put the tray in the freezer instead. Once frozen, transfer to a freezer bag and take them out when needed. Thoroughly defrost in the fridge before cooking.*

STEP 4

To cook, heat the oven to 200C/ 180 fan/ gas 6. Arrange as many as you need on a baking tray and cook for around 15 mins or until golden and cooked through. The inside will be very hot so make sure it's sufficiently cooled before serving to your little one.

Halloween toffee apples

Prep:20 mins **Cook:**10 mins

Serves 8

Ingredients

- 8 red apples
- 400g caster sugar
- 1 tsp lemon juice
- 4 tbsp golden syrup
- red or black food colouring
- red or black food glitter (optional)

You will need

- 8 sturdy, clean twigs or lolly sticks

Method

STEP 1

Pull any stalks off the twigs and push the sharpest end of each stick (or the lolly sticks) into the stalk-end of each apple, making sure it is firmly wedged in. Put a large piece of baking parchment onto a wooden board.

STEP 2

Tip the sugar into a large saucepan and add the lemon juice and 100ml water. Bring to a simmer and cook until the sugar has dissolved. Swirl the pan gently to move the sugar around, but don't stir. Add the golden syrup and bubble the mixture (be careful it doesn't boil over) until it reaches 'hard crack' stage or 150C on a sugar thermometer. If you don't have a thermometer, test the toffee by dropping a small amount into cold water. It should harden instantly and, when removed, be brittle. If it's soft, continue to boil. When it's ready, drip in some food colouring and swirl to combine. Add the glitter, if using, and turn off the heat.

STEP 3

Working quickly, dip each apple into the toffee, tipping the pan to cover all the skin. Lift out and allow any excess to drip off before putting on the baking parchment. Repeat with the remaining apples. Gently heat the toffee again if you need to. Best eaten on the same day.

Malted milk melting snowman cake

Prep: 1 hr **Cook:** 1 hr and 25 mins

Serves 25 - 30

Ingredients

For the sponges

- 500g unsalted butter , softened, plus extra for greasing
- 500g golden caster sugar
- 10 eggs
- 200g plain flour
- 200g full-fat natural yogurt
- 460g self-raising flour
- 4 tbsp malt extract (or 2 tbsp vanilla paste)
- 1 tbsp full-fat milk (or 2 tbsp if using vanilla paste)

For the buttercream

- 400g unsalted butter , softened
- 700g icing sugar
- 2 tbsp malt extract (or 1 tbsp vanilla paste)
- 1 tbsp full-fat milk

For the drippy ganache

- 100g white chocolate
- ½ tsp vegetable oil

To decorate

- 30g black fondant
- 30g bright orange fondant
- 1 wooden dowel , cut the same length as the nose
- 2-3 giant chocolate buttons
- 2 white chocolate Mikado sticks , for the arms

You will need

- 2 x 20cm cake tins
- 16cm hemisphere cake tin
- 23cm cake board
- 16cm cake board

- squeezy bottle

Method

STEP 1

Heat oven to 160C/140C fan/gas 3. Grease two 20cm round cake tins and line with baking parchment. Heavily grease a 16cm hemisphere cake tin and stand on a ramekin on a baking sheet to hold it steady.

STEP 2

First, make the sponges. Using electric beaters or a tabletop mixer, beat the butter and sugar together until pale and fluffy. Pour the eggs in, one at a time, giving the mix a thorough beating before adding the next. If the mix starts to look curdled, add 2 tbsp of the plain flour. Beat in the yogurt.

STEP 3

Mix both the flours together, adding ½ tsp salt, and slowly beat into the batter, followed by the malt extract (or vanilla paste) and milk. Spoon half the mixture into one of the 20cm tins, and split the remaining half between the other 20cm tin and the 16cm hemisphere. Bake the smaller amount of cake batter in the 20cm tin and the 16cm tin for 1 hr, and the larger amount for 1 hr 20 mins or until a skewer comes out clean when inserted into the middle of the cakes. Cool in the tin for 10 mins before turning out onto a wire rack to cool completely. *Can be frozen at this stage for up to three months.*

STEP 4

Meanwhile, make the buttercream by beating all the butter and half the icing sugar together using an electric whisk or tabletop mixer. Add the rest of the icing sugar once incorporated, followed by the malt extract (or vanilla paste) and milk. Set aside until ready to use.

STEP 5

To assemble, halve the largest 20cm cake horizontally so you are left with two equal-sized sponges the same size as the remaining 20cm cake. Put a blob of buttercream onto a 23cm cake board (or cake stand) and spread using a palette knife. Stick one of the sponges to the board. Spread a thick layer of buttercream on top of the cake and sandwich another sponge on top. Spread over another thick layer and sit the final sponge on top. Using a palette knife, coat the entire cake in a thin layer of buttercream and smooth the sides and top carefully, working around the whole cake, scraping off any excess icing. Chill in the freezer for 10 mins or in the fridge for 1 hr until set.

STEP 6

Meanwhile, put the hemisphere sponge on the smaller cake board and halve horizontally. Fill the middle with some buttercream, sandwich with the top and coat the entire cake in a thin layer of buttercream. Chill in the freezer for 5 mins or in the fridge for 30 mins.

STEP 7

Take the larger cake out of the fridge/ freezer and coat in another layer of buttercream. Take care when covering this time, as you want a smooth finish to the cake. Running the palette knife under hot water helps smooth over the sides once it is coated completely. Chill again for 5 mins in the freezer.

STEP 8

Cover the hemisphere sponge with buttercream and smooth over with the palette knife. Carefully lift the hemisphere onto the centre of the cake (as the sponge has been frozen you shouldn't leave finger marks). Press down lightly to set on the buttercream. If there is a gap around the rim, use a small palette knife to fill in with any remaining buttercream. Chill for 10-15 mins.

STEP 9

Meanwhile, make the eyes and nose using coloured fondant. Roll the black fondant into two balls for the eyes, and five smaller balls for the mouth. Roll the orange fondant into a carrot shape. Leave to set and harden slightly while you make the drippy ganache.

STEP 10

Make the drippy ganache by mixing the chocolate and oil and microwaving for 30 secs, stirring and then giving it another 30 secs until melted. Transfer to a squeezy bottle, then pour down the edges of the round cake to create the melting snow effect.

STEP 11

To finish the cake, stick the eyes to the head using a little remaining buttercream. Poke the wooden dowel into the carrot nose, leaving some poking out to stick it to the face. Stick the five small black fondant balls for the mouth and the chocolate buttons down the front of the cake for buttons. Insert the Mikado sticks on either side for the arms. Bring the cake to room temperature before serving.

Chicken schnitzel with coleslaw

Prep:30 mins **Cook:**10 mins

Serves 4

Ingredients

For the schnitzel

- 4 small chicken breasts
- 3 tbsp grated parmesan
- 100g flour
- 1 large egg , beaten
- 75g dried breadcrumbs (we used panko)
- 75ml vegetable oil

For the coleslaw

- 300g white cabbage , shredded
- 1 large carrot , peeled and grated
- 6 spring onions , sliced diagonally
- 1 red-skinned apple , grated
- 150g pot natural yogurt
- juice 0.5 lemon
- 2 tsp English mustard

Method

STEP 1

For the coleslaw, get your child to mix all the ingredients in a large bowl. Season a little and set aside.

STEP 2

Place a layer of cling film on your work surface and pop the chicken fillets on top. Cover with another piece of cling film and, using a rolling pin, ask your child to bash the chicken until it is 2-3mm thick.

STEP 3

Put the flour on a plate and season, then put the egg on another plate. Get your child to dip the chicken in the flour to coat, then into the egg.

STEP 4

Mix together the breadcrumbs and Parmesan in a shallow bowl, then ask your child to toss the chicken in the mixture to completely coat in the crumbs. Put the chicken on a plate and chill in the fridge until ready to eat if you're not cooking them straight away.

STEP 5

Heat the oil in a large frying pan over a fairly high heat and cook the chicken schnitzels two at a time. Sizzle them for 2-3 mins each side until completely golden, then lift out onto kitchen paper to drain. You can keep them warm in a low oven while you cook the rest. Serve with the coleslaw.

Orange and raspberry Hey Duggee cake

Prep:1 hr and 30 mins **Cook:**1 hr and 40 mins

Serves 16

Ingredients

For the cake

- 300g unsalted butter , room temperature
- 300g caster sugar
- 2 tsp vanilla extract
- 6 large eggs
- 400g self-raising flour
- 130g natural yogurt
- 2 tbsp milk (if needed)

For the syrup

- 50g caster sugar
- 1 tsp vanilla extract

For the orange buttercream & jam filling

- 250g unsalted butter , softened
- 550g icing sugar
- 75g orange curd
- 3 tbsp raspberry jam

For the decoration

- 500g red sugarpaste
- 250g yellow sugarpaste
- 140g blue sugarpaste
- 100g brown sugarpaste

- 25g black sugarpaste
- 80cm length of yellow ribbon (optional)

Method

STEP 1

Start by making the cake. Heat oven to 180C/160C fan/gas 4 and lightly grease a 23cm deep round cake pan, lining the base with parchment paper.

STEP 2

Cream the butter and sugar together in a large bowl using an electric hand whisk until light and fluffy – this should take about 10 mins. Add the vanilla and whisk again to combine. Beat the eggs a little with a fork, and with the beaters still running, add the eggs a little bit at a time. Wait until each addition has been fully combined before adding more.

STEP 3

Once all of the eggs have been added, fold in the flour with a spatula in three additions, alternating with the yogurt. If the finished batter feels a little stiff, mix in a couple tbsp of milk to loosen it. Transfer the batter into the prepared cake pan and level out with a spatula.

STEP 4

Bake in the preheated oven for about 1 hr 30 – 1 hr 40 mins or until a skewer inserted into the middle of the cake comes out clean. If the cake is browning too quickly, cover loosely with baking parchment for the last 15 mins of cooking. Allow the cake to cool in the tin for 20 mins.

STEP 5

While the cake is cooling in the tin make the syrup. Place the sugar, 50ml water and vanilla extract into a small saucepan over a medium heat and bring to a simmer, cooking for a few mins until the sugar has dissolved. Transfer the cake onto a wire rack to cool completely then use a skewer to poke holes all over the top of the cake. Use a pastry brush to spread the syrup over the top of the cake, allowing it to soak into the sponge before adding more.

STEP 6

To make the buttercream, beat the butter and icing sugar together with an electric hand whisk until light and fluffy, then add the orange curd and whisk again to combine. If the cake is domed on the top, use a large serrated knife to level it off then cut the cake through the middle, into two layers. Place the bottom layer of cake onto a 23cm round cake board and spread a thin layer of buttercream on the cake and top with the raspberry jam. Place the second layer of cake on top and spread the remaining buttercream over the top and sides of the cake.

STEP 7

On a work surface lightly dusted with icing sugar, knead the red sugarpaste until soft and pliable. Roll it out until about 3-4mm thick and wide enough to cover the cake. Roll the sugarpaste onto the rolling pin and carefully drape over the cake. Gently smooth the sugarpaste down the sides of the cake and trim off the excess with a small sharp knife. Reserve the trimmings for the details later on.

STEP 8

Repeat the rolling process with the yellow sugarpaste but this time cutting into thin strips. Cut 30 strips approx 1.5cm x 10cm and stick to the sides of the cake all the way around, dipping your finger in water to brush onto the back of each one, which will act as glue (the strips should cover the entire height of the cake but only reach a couple of centimetres over the top of cake).

STEP 9

Next roll out the blue sugarpaste to the same thickness as the red and yellow but this time cut out a 20cm circle and stick it in place in the middle of the cake using a little water. Roll out the brown sugarpaste as well and use a thin sharp knife to cut out Duggee's face and attach to the blue circle.

STEP 10

For Duggee's clothes knead a little yellow into the remaining brown sugarpaste until it is a light brown colour and use this to cut out his shirt and lip area, sticking with a little water as before. Use the black sugarpaste to roll his eyes and nose, using your hands rather than rolling on the work surface. Use the remaining sugarpaste to shape the decorations for his outfit and mouth and stick as before with a little water. Wrap the ribbon around the bottom edge of the cake and secure with tape or a pin but remember to remove before serving. *This cake will keep in a sealed container for up to 4 days.*

Mini Egg cake

Prep:1 hr and 15 mins **Cook:**45 mins

Serves 16

Ingredients

- 250g butter , softened, plus a little extra, melted, for the tin
- 250g self-raising flour , plus extra for dusting
- 225g golden caster sugar
- 2 oranges , zested
- 5 large eggs
- 1 tsp baking powder

For the drizzle

- 2 oranges , juiced (use the ones you've zested)

- 2 tbsp golden caster sugar

For the icing

- 150g butter , softened
- 500g icing sugar
- 1 tsp vanilla extract
- 180g tub full-fat cream cheese

For the decoration

- 4 x 90g bags Cadbury's Mini Eggs

Method

STEP 1

Heat oven to 180C/160C fan/gas 4. Butter a bundt tin or fluted cake ring (at least 2.5-litre capacity), then dust the tin with a little flour, shaking off the excess. Beat all the cake ingredients with a pinch of salt using an electric whisk until you have a smooth batter. Spoon into the prepared tin, smoothing the top with a palette knife, then bake for 35 mins until a skewer inserted into the centre comes out mostly clean with a few dry crumbs attached.

STEP 2

For the drizzle, combine the sugar with the orange juice in a saucepan, then reduce over a medium heat to a loose syrupy consistency. Prick the base of the cake all over with a skewer, then pour over half the syrup, adding the rest once it has been absorbed, Leave the cake to cool in the tin for 15 mins, then turn out onto a wire rack to cool completely.

STEP 3

While the cake is cooling, make the icing. Beat the butter with half the icing sugar and the vanilla extract until smooth and fluffy. Add the remaining icing sugar and the cream cheese and beat again until well combined – don't overbeat or the icing will become runny.

STEP 4

Spread a thin layer of the icing over the entire cake, taking care to get into all the crevices, then pop in the fridge for 20 mins to set. If you are short of time, you can always put it in the freezer. Spread the remaining icing onto the cake in an even layer. Once iced, the cake will keep in the fridge for three days. Bring to room temperature before decorating and serving.

STEP 5

Sort the Mini Eggs into different colours (a possibly therapeutic exercise, depending on your organisational tendencies). Stick the Mini Eggs all over the top of the cake.

Lunchbox pasta salad

Prep:15 mins **Cook:**11 mins

Serves 4

Ingredients

- 400g pasta
- 4-5 tbsp fresh pesto
- 1 tbsp mayonnaise
- 2 tbsp Greek yogurt
- ½ lemon , juiced
- 200g mixed cooked veg such as peas, green beans, courgette (chop the beans and courgette into pea-sized pieces)
- 100g cherry tomatoes , quartered
- 200g cooked chicken , ham, prawns, hard-boiled egg or cheese

Method

STEP 1

Cook the pasta in boiling water until it is al dente, so about 11 mins, but refer to the pack instructions. Drain and tip into a bowl. Stir in the pesto and leave to cool.

STEP 2

When the pasta is cool, stir through the mayo, yogurt, lemon juice and veg. Spoon into lunchboxes or on to pasta plates and put the cooked chicken or protein of your choice on top. Chill until ready to eat if intended for a packed lunch.

Mozzarella & salami picnic baguette

Prep:10 mins

Plus at least 1 hr resting

Serves 4

Ingredients

- 1 white or brown baguette
- 3 tbsp fresh green pesto
- 1 beef tomato
- 1 ball mozzarella (about 200g)

- 2 handfuls baby spinach leaves
- handful basil leaves
- 6 slices salami

Method

STEP 1

Slice the baguette in half lengthways and hollow out (make crumbs from the bread centre and save for another recipe). Spread the bottom half with the pesto. Slice the tomato and layer it over the pesto. Slice the mozzarella and add in a layer over the tomato.

STEP 2

Finish with layers of spinach and basil, plus the salami, folded in half if necessary to fit the width of the baguette.

STEP 3

Wrap in baking parchment, tie with string and pop in the fridge weighted under something heavy (we used a hefty griddle pan). Leave for at least 1 hr (or overnight if you like). The flavours will mingle and the sandwich will flatten down, making it a doddle to cut up without all the ingredients falling out all over your picnic rug.

Tex-Mex meatball tacos

Prep:25 mins **Cook:**10 mins

Serves 4

Ingredients

- 400g beef mince
- 1 egg
- 35g sachet fajita spice mix
- 4 large tomatoes , roughly chopped
- small bunch coriander , roughly chopped
- 1 garlic clove , crushed
- 2 limes , 1 juiced, 1 cut into wedges to serve
- 2 tbsp olive oil
- 150ml soured cream
- 75g grated cheddar or mozzarella
- 1 avocado
- 8 taco shells

Method

STEP 1

Mix the mince with the egg, spice mix and some seasoning, then shape into 16 meatballs. Set aside in the fridge to firm up slightly while you make the sides.

STEP 2

Mix the tomatoes, coriander, ½ the garlic and ½ the lime juice in a bowl with 1 tbsp oil, season and set aside. Stir the remaining garlic into the soured cream with a handful of the grated cheese and season. Slice the avocado and squeeze over the remaining lime juice. Bring these, the taco shells and lime wedges to the table.

STEP 3

Heat the remaining oil in a large frying pan. Fry the meatballs over a medium heat for 8-10 mins until evenly browned and cooked through. Sprinkle over the remaining cheese, put a lid on the pan and cook for 1 min until melted, then let everyone help themselves.

Winter wonderland cake

Prep:1 hr **Cook:**35 mins

Serves 12

Ingredients

- 175g unsalted butter , softened, plus more for the tin
- 250g golden caster sugar
- 3 large eggs
- 225g plain flour
- 2 tsp baking powder
- 50g crème fraîche
- 100g dark chocolate , melted and cooled a little
- 3 tbsp strawberry jam
- 8-10 candy canes , red and white
- mini white meringues and jelly sweets, to decorate

For the angel frosting

- 500g white caster sugar
- 1 tsp vanilla extract
- 1 tbsp liquid glucose
- 2 egg whites

- 30g icing sugar , sifted

Method

STEP 1

Heat oven to 180C/160C fan/gas 4. Butter and line three 18cm (or two 20cm) cake tins. Beat the butter and sugar together until light and fluffy. Add the eggs, beating them in one at a time. Fold in the flour, baking powder and a pinch of salt, then fold in the crème fraîche and chocolate and 100ml boiling water.

STEP 2

Divide the cake mixture between the tins and level the tops of the batter. Bake for 25-30 mins or until a skewer inserted into the middle comes out clean. Leave to cool for 10 mins in the tin, then tip out onto a cooling rack and peel off the parchment. Set aside to cool completely.

STEP 3

To make the angel frosting, put the sugar, vanilla and liquid glucose in a pan with 125ml water. Bring to the boil and cook until the sugar has melted – the syrup turns clear and the mixture hits 130C on a sugar thermometer (be very careful with hot sugar). Take off the heat. Meanwhile, beat the egg whites until stiff then, while still beating, gradually pour in the hot sugar syrup in a steady stream. Keep beating until the mixture is fluffy and thick enough to spread – this might take a few mins as the mixture cools. Beat in the icing sugar.

STEP 4

Spread two of the sponges with jam and some of the icing mixture, then sandwich the cakes together with the plain one on top. Use a little of the frosting to ice the whole cake (don't worry about crumbs at this stage). Use the remaining icing to ice the cake again, smoothing the side, and swirling it on top. Crush four of the candy canes and sprinkle over the cake, then add the remaining whole candy canes, meringues and sweets.

Halloween biscuits

Prep:45 mins **Cook:**25 mins

Serves 7 - 8

Ingredients

For the biscuits

- 200g unsalted butter , softened
- 200g golden caster sugar
- 1 large egg

- ½ tsp vanilla extract
- 400g plain flour , plus extra for dusting
- 20g popping candy (or rainbow sprinkles for very young children)

For decoration

- White, black and grey sugar paste
- 100g icing sugar

Method

STEP 1

Heat oven to 200C/180C fan/gas 6 and line a baking sheet with baking parchment.

STEP 2

Put the butter in a bowl and beat with electric beaters until soft and creamy. Beat in the sugar, then the egg and vanilla, and finally the flour to make a dough. If the dough feels a bit sticky add a little more flour and knead it in. Wrap in cling film and put in the fridge for half an hour.

STEP 3

Heavily flour a surface and cut the pastry in half. Roll out one half to 5mm thickness. Using a cookie cutter in the shape of a ghost (or any spooky shaped cutter you like), cut out 12 ghost shapes, which will make 4 cookies. Put the cut shapes on a baking tray lined with baking paper and put back in the fridge. Repeat with the second half of the pastry. Swap into the fridge, taking the chilled ghost biscuits out.

STEP 4

Using a smaller cutter or a knife, cut a ghost-shaped hole in the middle of 4 of the biscuits on the tray, this is the space to store the surprise centre! Put these biscuits into the oven to bake for 10-12 mins, until pale but cooked through. Transfer to a wire rack to cool. Repeat with the other tray.

STEP 5

Once all the biscuits have cooled completely, they are ready to be assembled. Mix the icing sugar with 3 tbsp of water and mix well. It should be quite thick so add a little more icing sugar if the mixture is too runny. Take a biscuit without the centre missing, and spread or pipe a little icing around the edge. Press a biscuit with a centre missing on top, then sprinkle popping candy into the pocket that you have created (*or rainbow sprinkles as an alternative, if you're serving to very young children*). Spread icing on the edge of the second biscuit and press another whole biscuit on top. Set aside to firm up. Make sure you leave them for a while so they don't slide when you are finishing the decoration.

STEP 6

Once the biscuits feel firm and the icing has set, use the sugar paste to decorate them as you please, rolling it out, cutting it to shape and topping the biscuits. You may have to use a little of the icing to glue it down. Decorate with icing pens if you like.

Rice paper wraps

Prep:20 mins **Cook:**3 mins

Serves 8

Ingredients

- 50g rice vermicelli noodles
- 1 carrot , peeled
- 1 avocado , peeled and destoned
- ¼ cucumber
- 8 rice paper wraps
- 8 king prawns , peeled and cooked
- 8 mint leaves
- ½ cooked chicken breast, shredded
- sweet chilli sauce , to serve

Method

STEP 1

Put the noodles in a pan of water and bring to the boil, simmer for 3 mins, then cool under running water. Drain thoroughly.

STEP 2

Cut the carrot into matchsticks using a knife or a mandoline. Cut the avocado into strips and the cucumber into thin sticks. Soak 2 of the rice paper wraps in cold water for 1-2 mins until floppy.

STEP 3

Lift 1 sheet of rice paper out of the water, shake gently, then lay it carefully on a board. Place 2 prawns in the centre, with a mint leaf between them. Add a strip of avocado, pile some noodles on top, then add a layer of carrot and cucumber. Fold the bottom half of the rice paper over, then fold the sides in and tightly roll it up. Repeat using the second wrapper and soak 2 more to make 2 more rolls.

STEP 4

Make the rest of the rolls up using the remaining 4 wraps and the shredded chicken instead of prawns. Serve the rolls with the sweet chilli sauce for dipping.

Fluffy pancakes

Prep:10 mins **Cook:**20 mins

Makes 6

Ingredients

- 8 slices pancetta, to serve (optional)
- sunflower oil and butter, for cooking
- blueberries, to serve (optional)

For the pancakes

- 300g self-raising flour
- 1 tsp baking powder
- 1 tbsp caster sugar
- 2 medium eggs
- 1 tbsp maple syrup, plus extra to serve
- 300ml milk

Method

STEP 1

If serving with pancetta, heat oven to 200C/180C fan/gas 6. Line a baking tray with baking parchment and lay on the pancetta in a single layer. Put another piece of parchment on top, followed by a second baking tray, and bake for 12-15 mins until crisp.

STEP 2

To make the pancakes, get a little helper to weigh out and tip the flour, baking powder and sugar into a large bowl with a small pinch of salt. Crack in the eggs and whisk until smooth. Add the maple syrup and milk while whisking.

STEP 3

Heat a splash of oil and a small knob of butter in a non-stick frying pan until sizzling. Add spoonfuls of batter to make pancakes the size you like, we made 20cm pancakes for a serving size of one per person, or if you are very hungry, two per person. Cook until bubbles start to form on the surface, then flip and cook the other side. Eat straight away or keep warm in a low oven while you cook another batch. Serve pancakes with pancetta or blueberries, drizzled with extra maple syrup.

Christmas stollen with almonds & marzipan

Prep: 1 hr and 25 mins **Cook:** 1 hr and 15 mins

Plus soaking, 2-3 hrs proving, and cooling

Cuts into 10 slices

Ingredients

- 100g mixed dried fruit with peel
- 180ml apple juice
- 7g dried yeast
- 250g plain flour , plus a little extra for dusting
- 30g blanched whole almonds
- generous pinch of ground cinnamon
- generous pinch of ground aniseed or allspice
- small pinch of ground cloves
- 75g cold marzipan , cut into small pieces
- 10g butter , melted
- 1 tbsp icing sugar

Method

STEP 1

Soak the dried fruit in 100ml of hot water. Gently warm the apple juice for a few mins in a pan, then add the yeast and leave to activate for 10-15 mins (it will start to bubble).

STEP 2

Put the flour in a bowl. Stir in the yeast and apple juice mixture to form a smooth dough, then cover and leave to prove somewhere warm until roughly doubled in size, about 1-2 hrs. You can also put the dough in the fridge to rise slowly overnight.

STEP 3

Drain the fruit and add to the dough along with the nuts, spices and marzipan. Squish everything together, then turn the dough out onto a lightly floured work surface and knead until the fruit stays in the dough.

STEP 4

Shape the dough into a sausage shape and put it on a baking tray lined with baking parchment. Cover with a clean tea towel and leave to prove somewhere warm for 30 mins–1 hr until it has risen by about a quarter.

STEP 5

Heat oven to 180C/160C fan/gas 4. Bake the stollen for 20 mins, then reduce oven to 150C/130C fan/gas 2 and bake for 25-30 mins more until golden brown and firm to the touch.

STEP 6

Remove the stollen from the oven and brush all over with the melted butter. Dust with the icing sugar and leave to cool completely before slicing. Store any remaining stollen, well wrapped, in an airtight container.

Chicken satay

Prep:30 mins **Cook:**10 mins

Makes 12

Ingredients

- small piece ginger
- 2 garlic cloves
- zest and juice 1 lime
- 1 tsp clear honey
- 1 tbsp soy sauce
- 1 tbsp mild curry powder
- 3 tbsp smooth peanut butter
- 500g pack skinless chicken breast fillets
- 165ml can coconut milk
- 1 tsp vegetable oil
- cooked rice and lime wedges, to serve

For the cucumber salad

- 1 cucumber
- 2 tbsp white wine vinegar
- 1 tbsp golden caster sugar
- sweet chilli sauce (optional)
- bunch coriander leaves picked (optional)

Method

STEP 1

KIDS the writing in bold is for you. GROWN-UPS the rest is for you. **Make a yummy marinade.** Peel the ginger and help them to finely grate it and tip it into a bowl. Repeat with the garlic and lime zest. Halve the lime and get your child to juice it, then mix it in a bowl with the honey, soy, curry powder and peanut butter. Get them to give it a good mix, adding a small splash of water if it's too stiff, then help them spoon two-thirds of the mix into a small pan. Set aside for Step 4.

STEP 2

Now for some chicken bashing! Put the chicken in the sandwich bag, one breast at a time, getting your child to flatten each one with a rolling pin or a meat mallet – this isn't essential, but they like doing it.

STEP 3

Mix the chicken with the marinade you made. Cut the chicken into strips, tip it into the remaining third of the peanut-butter mix, then get your child to stir well. Cover with cling film and chill until required. *This can be done up to 3 hrs ahead.*

STEP 4

Cook your tasty sauce. While the chicken is marinating, pour the coconut milk into the pan and get your child to stir together with the peanut butter mix. The sauce needs to be heated gently and stirred – suitable for confident seven- or eight-year olds, under strict adult supervision.

STEP 5

'Sew' the chicken onto the skewers. The chicken needs to be threaded into 'S' shapes onto the skewers. Get your child to thread the skewers away from themselves, being careful of the sharp points. Younger ones might find this a little fiddly, so they could just push on small chunks.

STEP 6

Paint the tray with oil and cook the chicken. Heat the grill to high and get your child to brush a baking tray with oil. They can then line up the skewers on the tray. Grill the skewers for about 10 mins, turning occasionally, until lightly charred.

STEP 7

Make cucumber ribbons with a peeler. Using a swivel-blade peeler, get your child to peel the cucumber into a bowl, then carry on peeling the cucumber flesh into ribbons until they get to the seeds. Repeat with each side of the cucumber.

STEP 8

Mix a dressing for the cucumber. Get your child to mix the vinegar and sugar until the sugar dissolves – explain what dissolves means. Add the sweet chilli, if using, then pour over the cucumber. Add coriander if your child likes it, or serve on the side for the grown-ups. To serve, put the skewers on a platter, the sauce and salad in bowls, and serve with rice and lime wedges on the side.

Pudsey biscuits

Prep:1 hr **Cook:**20 mins

Makes around 20 biscuits

Ingredients

- 200g unsalted butter , softened
- 200g golden caster sugar
- 1 large egg
- ½ tsp vanilla extract
- 400g plain flour , plus extra for dusting

To decorate

- 25g icing sugar
- 50g white fondant
- coloured icing pens (writing quality)
- 25g black sugar paste
- hundreds and thousands or sweets to decorate (optional)

Method

STEP 1

Heat oven to 200C/180C fan/gas 6 and line a baking sheet with baking parchment. Put the butter in a bowl and beat it with electric beaters until soft and creamy. Beat in the sugar, then the egg and vanilla, and finally the flour to make a dough. If the dough feels a bit sticky, add a little bit more flour and knead it in.

STEP 2

Roll the dough out so it's about the thickness of a £1 coin. Cut out shapes using a Pudsey bear cutter or cut around a template you have made. Re-roll off-cuts and repeat.

STEP 3

Transfer the biscuits to the baking sheet and bake for 8-10 mins or until the edges are just brown. Leave to cool completely.

STEP 4

To decorate the biscuits: Mix the icing sugar with enough water to make a stiff paste then roll the white fondant out to 5mm thick and cut into strips to make Pudsey's eye bandage. Stick it on with the white icing. Decorate with polka dots using coloured icing pens. Make his eye, nose and mouth with the black sugar paste and add a little dot of white icing to the eye. Stick the features down with more icing. Repeat the process with most of the biscuits and decorate the rest with icing simply sprinkled with hundreds and thousands. Will keep for three days in a biscuit tin.

White rabbit biscuits

Prep:1 hr and 10 mins **Cook:**45 mins

Makes 30-35 biscuits or 15 bunnies

Ingredients

- 200g unsalted butter , at room temperature
- 400g plain flour
- 280g caster sugar
- 1 egg
- ¼ tsp vanilla extract
- a pinch of salt
- ½ tsp cream of tartar

For the icing:

- 600g icing sugar
- pink food colouring gel
- 170g pack of desiccated coconut
- 15 mini marshmallows

You will also need:

- 1 x rabbit head-shaped cookie cutter
- 1 x 7cm round cookie cutter
- 1 x 3cm round cookie cutter

Method

STEP 1

Heat oven to 180C/160C fan/gas 4. Lightly rub the butter and flour together with your fingertips until the mixture looks like fresh breadcrumbs.

STEP 2

Mix the sugar and egg together in another in a bowl with a whisk and when it is really well combined and runny add it to the flour mixture.

STEP 3

Add all the other ingredients and squish it together with your hands, keep working the dough until it's smooth, soft and comes together in one piece.

STEP 4

Roll the dough out on a lightly floured surface with a rolling pin until it is about half a centimetre thick. Cut into shapes. We did 15 rabbit heads, 15 large circles and 30 mini circles.

STEP 5

Place your biscuits on baking sheets lined with baking paper and bake in batches for about 15 mins (or until they are lightly golden at the edges).

STEP 6

Let them cool in the tin for a few minutes before carefully transferring them to a wire rack to cool completely and become crisp.

STEP 7

While the biscuits cool mix enough cold water with the icing sugar to create a thick icing. Place a quarter of the icing in another bowl and add a very small amout of pink gel food colouring. Transfer both the white icing and the pink icing into disposable piping bags and snip off the end to make a very small nozzle on the pink icing and a wider one on the white icing.

STEP 8

Pipe white icing over the small round biscuits and leave to dry. Then pipe white icing to cover all of the large circular biscuits and the rabbit biscuits (be fairly sparing and spread it out with the back of a spoon – it doesn't have to be neat on these ones). Once you've iced each one sprinkle generously with dessicated coconut before the icing dries.

STEP 9

Take the pink icing and use to create paws on the smaller circles then stick 2 of them onto each of the large circles using icing like glue. With the icing you have left, coat the marshmallows and cover those in coconut too before sticking them onto the middle of the larger circles to create a fluffy tail. Leave to set completely for about 15-20 mins then serve.

Sam's toad-in-the-hole

Prep:15 mins **Cook:**45 mins

Serves 4

Ingredients

- 12 chipolatas
- 1 tbsp sunflower oil

For the batter

- 140g plain flour
- 2 eggs
- 175ml semi-skimmed milk

Method

STEP 1

Heat the oven to 220C/200C fan/gas 7. Put the chipolatas in a 20 x 30cm roasting tin with the oil and bake for 15 mins until browned.

STEP 2

Meanwhile, make the batter. Tip the flour into a bowl with ½ tsp salt, make a well in the middle and crack the eggs into it. Use an electric whisk to mix it together, then slowly add the milk, whisking all the time. Leave to stand until the sausages are nice and brown.

STEP 3

Remove the sausages from the oven – be careful because the fat will be sizzling hot – but if it isn't, put the tin on the hob for a few minutes until it is.

STEP 4

Pour in the batter mix, transfer to the top shelf of the oven, then cook for 25-30 mins, until risen and golden. Serve with gravy and your favourite veg.

Red cabbage & pickled chilli slaw

Prep: 10 mins

Serves 8

Ingredients

- 1 small red cabbage (about 500g), finely shredded
- 1 red onion , thinly sliced
- 3 medium carrots (about 150g each), coarsely grated
- 2 tbsp chopped pickled jalapeño chillies , plus 100ml of their pickling liquid
- 1 lime , juiced (optional)

Method

STEP 1

Put the cabbage and onion in a bowl, season with salt and a small pinch of sugar and leave for 30 mins.

STEP 2

Stir the carrot, jalapeños and their pickling liquid through the cabbage. If making ahead, prep the vegetables but don't season or dress until the last minute.

Broccoli & potato croquettes

Prep:15 mins **Cook:**30 mins

makes 12

Ingredients

- 400g floury potatoes , large ones cut in half
- 150g broccoli , broken into florets
- 1medium egg yolk
- 40g mature cheddar , grated
- 60g fresh breadcrumbs

For the crust

- 20g plain flour
- 2 medium eggs , beaten
- 100g sesame seeds
- 4 tbsp olive oil

For the dip

- 100g cream cheese
- 50g natural yogurt
- 1 tbsp chives , snipped
- 1-2 tbsp full-fat milk , if needed

Method

STEP 1

Put the potatoes in a medium saucepan and just cover with cold water. Bring to the boil and simmer for 14-16 mins until completely cooked through. Drain and mash well, then put back in the saucepan over a low heat and cook for 1-2 mins, stirring constantly – this will remove excess moisture.

STEP 2

Meanwhile, bring a small saucepan of water to the boil, add the broccoli and simmer for 6-7 mins until tender. Drain really well and pat dry with kitchen paper (it's important to do this thoroughly as excess water will make the croquettes a little wet). Finely chop the broccoli, then add to the mashed potato with the egg yolk, cheese and breadcrumbs. Divide the mixture into 12 equal balls and roll each one into a short sausage shape. Chill for 10 mins in the freezer.

STEP 3

Meanwhile, make the dip. Put the cream cheese, yogurt and chives in a bowl and stir to a soft consistency, adding the milk if needed.

STEP 4

Put the flour, beaten eggs and sesame seeds in three separate bowls. Roll the croquettes in the flour, dip in the beaten egg, then roll in the sesame seeds.

STEP 5

Heat the oil in a large, non-stick frying pan and fry the croquettes on a low-medium heat for 4-5 mins, turning frequently for an even, golden colour. Drain on kitchen paper and serve with the cream cheese dip.

Bread in four easy steps

Prep:15 mins **Cook:**35 mins

Plus rising

Easy

Cuts into 8 thick slices

Ingredients

- 500g granary, strong wholewheat or white bread flour (I used granary)
- 7g sachet fast-action dried yeast
- 1 tsp salt
- 2 tbsp olive oil
- 1 tbsp clear honey

Method

STEP 1

Tip the flour, yeast and salt into a large bowl and mix together with your hands. Stir 300ml hand-hot water with the oil and honey, then stir into the dry ingredients to make a soft dough.

STEP 2

Turn the dough out onto a lightly floured surface and knead for 5 mins, until the dough no longer feels sticky, sprinkling with a little more flour if you need it.

STEP 3

Oil a 900g loaf tin and put the dough in the tin, pressing it in evenly. Put in a large plastic food bag and leave to rise for 1 hr, until the dough has risen to fill the tin and it no longer springs back when you press it with your finger.

STEP 4

Heat oven to 200C/fan 180C/gas 6. Make several slashes across the top of the loaf with a sharp knife, then bake for 30-35 mins until the loaf is risen and golden. Tip it out onto a cooling rack and tap the base of the bread to check it is cooked. It should sound hollow. Leave to cool.

Chocolate fudge cupcakes

Prep:30 mins **Cook:**25 mins - 30 mins

Plus cooling

Easy

Makes 12

Ingredients

- 200g butter
- 200g plain chocolate , under 70% cocoa solids is fine
- 200g light, soft brown sugar
- 2 eggs , beaten
- 1 tsp vanilla extract

- 250g self-raising flour
- Smarties , sweets and sprinkles, to decorate

For the icing

- 200g plain chocolate
- 100ml double cream , not fridge-cold
- 50g icing sugar

Method

STEP 1

Heat oven to 160C/140C fan/gas 3 and line a 12-hole muffin tin with cases. Gently melt the butter, chocolate, sugar and 100ml hot water together in a large saucepan, stirring occasionally, then set aside to cool a little while you weigh the other ingredients.

STEP 2

Stir the eggs and vanilla into the chocolate mixture. Put the flour into a large mixing bowl, then stir in the chocolate mixture until smooth. Spoon into cases until just over three-quarters full (you may have a little mixture leftover), then set aside for 5 mins before putting on a low shelf in the oven and baking for 20-22 mins. Leave to cool.

STEP 3

For the icing, melt the chocolate in a heatproof bowl over a pan of barely simmering water. Once melted, turn off the heat, stir in the double cream and sift in the icing sugar. When spreadable, top each cake with some and decorate with your favourite sprinkles and sweets.

Bespoke martini kit

Easy

Ingredients

- 700ml bottle rye vodka
- small pot of juniper berries
- small pod of green cardamom pods
- small pot of dried rose petals
- small pot of coriander seeds

- 1 lemon
- 1 coffee filter paper
- bottle of vermouth
- small jar of green olives

Optional extras

- 2 martini glasses
- shot measure
- tall glass
- cocktail stirrer
- cocktail strainer

Method

STEP 1

To use the kit: *Write the following instructions on the gift tag:*
Open the bottle of vodka and add 2 tbsp juniper berries, 6 cardamom pods, a pinch of dried rose petals, 1 tsp coriander seeds and a strip of lemon peel. Put the lid back on and leave in a cool dark place for 24 hrs.

STEP 2

Strain the infused mixture through the coffee filter paper into a jug, then pour back into the bottle to store.

STEP 3

To make a martini, chill 2 martini glasses in the fridge for 30 mins. Put 50ml vermouth in a tall glass, add 150ml infused vodka and a large handful of ice. Stir well until the outside of the glass feels cold, then strain into the chilled glasses. Garnish with an olive.

Cheese, ham & grape kebabs

Prep: 10 mins

No cook

Easy

Serves 1

Ingredients

- 6 bocconcini (mini mozzarella balls)
- 6 grapes (a combination of red and green looks nice),
- 6 cubes of ham

Method

STEP 1

Using 3 short wooden skewers, thread on the mini mozzarella balls, grapes, and cubes of ham. Place in a sealable container or wrap in cling film and pop in a lunchbox.

White rabbit biscuits

Prep:1 hr and 10 mins **Cook:**45 mins

Easy

Makes 30-35 biscuits or 15 bunnies

Ingredients

- 200g unsalted butter , at room temperature
- 400g plain flour
- 280g caster sugar
- 1 egg
- ¼ tsp vanilla extract
- a pinch of salt
- ½ tsp cream of tartar

For the icing:

- 600g icing sugar
- pink food colouring gel
- 170g pack of desiccated coconut
- 15 mini marshmallows

You will also need:

- 1 x rabbit head-shaped cookie cutter
- 1 x 7cm round cookie cutter
- 1 x 3cm round cookie cutter

Method

STEP 1

Heat oven to 180C/160C fan/gas 4. Lightly rub the butter and flour together with your fingertips until the mixture looks like fresh breadcrumbs.

STEP 2

Mix the sugar and egg together in another in a bowl with a whisk and when it is really well combined and runny add it to the flour mixture.

STEP 3

Add all the other ingredients and squish it together with your hands, keep working the dough until it's smooth, soft and comes together in one piece.

STEP 4

Roll the dough out on a lightly floured surface with a rolling pin until it is about half a centimetre thick. Cut into shapes. We did 15 rabbit heads, 15 large circles and 30 mini circles.

STEP 5

Place your biscuits on baking sheets lined with baking paper and bake in batches for about 15 mins (or until they are lightly golden at the edges).

STEP 6

Let them cool in the tin for a few minutes before carefully transferring them to a wire rack to cool completely and become crisp.

STEP 7

While the biscuits cool mix enough cold water with the icing sugar to create a thick icing. Place a quarter of the icing in another bowl and add a very small amout of pink gel food colouring. Transfer both the white icing and the pink icing into disposable piping bags and snip off the end to make a very small nozzle on the pink icing and a wider one on the white icing.

STEP 8

Pipe white icing over the small round biscuits and leave to dry. Then pipe white icing to cover all of the large circular biscuits and the rabbit biscuits (be fairly sparing and spread it out with the back of a spoon – it doesn't have to be neat on these ones). Once you've iced each one sprinkle generously with dessicated coconut before the icing dries.

STEP 9

Take the pink icing and use to create paws on the smaller circles then stick 2 of them onto each of the large circles using icing like glue. With the icing you have left, coat the marshmallows and cover those in coconut too before sticking them onto the middle of the larger circles to create a fluffy tail. Leave to set completely for about 15-20 mins then serve.

Winter warmer hearty risotto

Prep:10 mins **Cook:**50 mins

Easy

Serves 4

Ingredients

- 1 medium butternut squash
- 2 tbsp olive oil
- pinch of nutmeg , or pinch of cinnamon
- 1 red onion , finely chopped
- 1 vegetable stock cube
- 2 garlic cloves , crushed
- 500g risotto rice (we used arborio)
- 100g frozen peas
- 320g sweetcorn , drained
- 2 tbsp grated parmesan (or vegetarian alternative)
- handful chopped mixed herbs of your choice

Method

STEP 1

Heat oven to 200C/180C fan/gas 6. Peel the butternut squash, slice it in half, then scoop out and discard the seeds.

STEP 2

Cut the flesh of the butternut squash into small cubes and put in a mixing bowl. Drizzle 1 tbsp olive oil over the squash, and season with black pepper, and nutmeg or cinnamon. Transfer the squash to a roasting tin and roast in the oven for about 25 mins until cooked through, then set aside.

STEP 3

Heat the remaining oil in a large saucepan over a low heat. Add the onion and cover the pan with a tight-fitting lid. Allow the onion to cook without colouring for 5-10 mins, stirring occasionally.

STEP 4

In a measuring jug, make up 1.5 litres of stock from boiling water and the stock cube. Stir well until the stock cube has dissolved. When the onion is soft, remove the lid and add the garlic to the onion pan. Leave it to cook for 1 min more.

STEP 5

Rinse the rice under cold water. Turn up the heat on the pan and add the rice to the onion and garlic, stirring well for 1 min. Pour a little of the hot stock into the pan and stir in until the liquid is absorbed by the rice.

STEP 6

Gradually add the rest of the stock to the pan, a little at a time, stirring constantly, waiting until each addition of stock is absorbed before adding more. Do this until the rice is cooked through and creamy – you may not need all the stock. This should take 15-20 mins. Take the roasting tin out of the oven – the squash should be soft and cooked.

STEP 7

Add the squash, peas and sweetcorn to the risotto and gently stir it in. Season to taste. Take the risotto pan off the heat and stir in the Parmesan and herbs. Put the lid back on the pan and let the risotto stand for 2-3 mins before serving.

Sausage plait

Prep:30 mins **Cook:**40 mins

Easy

Serves 4

Ingredients

- a little oil, for greasing
- 400g pack pork and apple sausage - about 6 fat sausages
- 1 roasted red pepper from a jar, patted dry with kitchen paper
- 1 large egg
- ½ tsp chilli flakes (optional)
- 2 tbsp tomato purée
- flour, for dusting
- 250g ready-made puff pastry
- baked beans or salad, to serve

Method

STEP 1

Heat oven to 200C/180C fan/ gas 6. Grease a baking tray with oil using a pastry brush, then cover it with baking parchment. Put to one side. Remove the meat from the sausage skins by snipping off the ends, then squeezing the sausagemeat into a bowl (see step 1).

STEP 2

Cut the pepper into small pieces with scissors. Break the egg into the cup, beat with a fork, and save 2 tbsp for glazing. Add the red pepper and remaining egg to the sausagemeat with the chilli flakes, if using, and purée. Mix well with a fork or clean hands (step 2).

STEP 3

Sprinkle some flour on the work surface. Using a rolling pin, roll out the pastry into a rough square shape, about 30 x 30cm. Put the pastry on the lined baking tray (step 3).

STEP 4

Now spoon the filling down the middle of the pastry in a sausage shape – leave a little gap at the top and bottom (about 3cm) (step 4).

STEP 5

Cut the pastry at a slight diagonal, on either side of the filling, into 1.5cm strips, the same number each side – we cut 12 strips each side. Brush the pastry all over with most of the saved egg (step 5).

STEP 6

Tuck the top and bottom edges of the pastry over the filling. Starting at the top, lay the pastry strips over the filling, taking one from each side, to cross like a plait. Now brush the top all over with the last of the egg. Bake for 35-40 mins or until golden. Serve hot or cold with baked beans or salad (step 6).

RECIPE TIPS

FOR PARENTS

This is an excellent recipe for children of all ages, as it doesn't require any sharp knives. Smaller children may need help using scissors and rolling the pastry to the desired shape, but don't worry if it doesn't look perfect – it will still taste great!

EQUIPMENT YOU NEED

Baking tray Pastry brush Baking parchment Kitchen scissors Large mixing bowl Kitchen paper Cup Fork, large spoon and cutlery knife Measuring spoons Rolling pin Ruler Oven gloves

BEFORE YOU START

Wash your hands, tie back long hair, if necessary, and put on an apron.

Simple sushi

Prep:40 mins **Cook:**15 mins

plus draining and 3 hrs cooling

Easy

Makes enough sushi for 6 as a main, or 4 with leftovers for lunchboxes

Ingredients

For the rice

- 300g sushi rice
- 100ml rice wine vinegar
- 2 tbsp golden caster sugar

For the Japanese mayonnaise

- 3 tbsp mayonnaise
- 1 tbsp rice wine vinegar
- 1 tsp soy sauce

For the sushi

- 25g bag nori (seaweed) sheets
- choose from the following fillings: cucumber strips, smoked salmon, white crabmeat, canned tuna, red pepper, avocado, spring onion

To serve with all styles of sushi

- wasabi (optional - and fiery!)
- pickled ginger
- soy sauce

Method

STEP 1

KIDS the writing in bold is for you. ADULTS the rest is for you. TO MAKE SUSHI ROLLS: **Pat out some rice.** Lay a nori sheet on the mat, shiny-side down. Dip your hands in the vinegared water, then pat handfuls of rice on top in a 1cm thick layer, leaving the furthest edge from you clear.

STEP 2

Spread over some Japanese mayonnaise. Use a spoon to spread out a thin layer of mayonnaise down the middle of the rice.

STEP 3

Add the filling. Get your child to top the mayonnaise with a line of their favourite fillings – here we've used tuna and cucumber.

STEP 4

Roll it up. Lift the edge of the mat over the rice, applying a little pressure to keep everything in a tight roll.

STEP 5

Stick down the sides like a stamp. When you get to the edge without any rice, brush with a little water and continue to roll into a tight roll.

STEP 6

Wrap in cling film. Remove the mat and roll tightly in cling film before a grown-up cuts the sushi into thick slices, then unravel the cling film.

STEP 7

TO MAKE PRESSED SUSHI: **Layer over some smoked salmon.** Line a loaf tin with cling film, then place a thin layer of smoked salmon inside on top of the cling film.

STEP 8

Cover with rice and press down. Press about 3cm of rice over the fish, fold the cling film over and press down as much as you can, using another tin if you have one.

STEP 9

Tip it out like a sandcastle. Turn block of sushi onto a chopping board. Get a grown-up to cut into fingers, then remove the cling film.

STEP 10

TO MAKE SUSHI BALLS: **Choose your topping.** Get a small square of cling film and place a topping, like half a prawn or a small piece of smoked salmon, on it. Use damp hands to roll walnut-sized balls of rice and place on the topping.

STEP 11

Make into tight balls. Bring the corners of the cling film together and tighten into balls by twisting it up, then unwrap and serve.

Blackberry & apple loaf

Total time2 hrs

Ready in 2 hours, including baking

Easy

Cuts into 10 chunky slices

Ingredients

- 250g self-raising flour
- 175g butter
- 175g light muscovado sugar
- ½ tsp cinnamon
- 2rounded tbsp demerara sugar
- 1 small eating apple, such as Cox's, quartered (not cored or peeled)

* 2 large eggs, beaten
* 1 orange, finely grated zest
* 1 tsp baking powder
* 225g blackberry

Method

STEP 1

Preheat the oven to 180C/gas 4/fan 160C. Butter and line the bottom of a 1.7 litre loaf tin (see tip below). In a large bowl, rub the flour, butter and muscovado sugar together with your fingers to make fine crumbs. Measure out 5 level tbsp of this mixture into a small bowl for the topping, and mix in to it the cinnamon and demerara sugar. Set aside.

STEP 2

Coarsely grate the apple down to the core and mix in with the eggs and the zest. Stir the baking powder into the rubbed-in mixture in the large bowl, then quickly and lightly stir in the egg mixture until it drops lightly from the spoon. Don't overmix.

STEP 3

Gently fold in three quarters of the berries with a metal spoon, trying not to break them up. Spoon into the tin and level. Scatter the rest of the berries on top. Sprinkle over the topping and bake for 1¼ -1 hour 20 minutes. Check after 50 minutes and cover loosely with foil if it is browning too much. When done the cake will feel firm, but test with a skewer.

STEP 4

Leave in the tin for 30 minutes before turning out, then cool on a wire rack. Peel off the paper before cutting. Will keep wrapped in foil or in a tin for up to 2 days.

RECIPE TIPS

WATCHING THE TIME

A 9x20x13cm loaf tin is ideal, but if yours is shallower, the cake may cook faster, so test after an hour.

Prawn & mango salad

Prep: 10 mins

No cook

Easy

Serves 2

Ingredients

- ½ avocado , peeled and cut into cubes, see tip, below left
- squeeze of lemon juice
- 50g small cooked prawns
- 1 mango cheek, peeled and cut into cubes
- 4 cherry tomatoes , halved
- finger-sized piece cucumber , chopped
- handful baby spinach leaves
- couple of mint leaves , very finely shredded
- 1-2 tsp sweet chilli sauce

Method

STEP 1

Mix the avocado with the lemon juice, then toss with the prawns, mango, tomatoes, cucumber, spinach and mint. Pack into a lunchbox and drizzle over the sweet chilli sauce, then chill until ready to eat.

Chocolate marble pancakes

Prep:10 mins **Cook:**10 mins

Easy

makes 12

Ingredients

- 200g self-raising flour
- 2 eggs
- 2 tbsp caster sugar
- 300ml whole milk
- 1 tsp vanilla extract
- 2 tbsp cocoa powder
- oil for frying
- chocolate sauce , to serve

Method

STEP 1

Put the flour, eggs and sugar into a bowl. Pour in the milk and whisk until you have a smooth batter, then divide in half. To one half of the batter, whisk in the vanilla extract, and to the other half, whisk in the cocoa powder.

STEP 2

Lightly oil a non-stick pan, set over a medium heat. Using two spoons, alternately drop the white and dark batter on top of each other, a little off centre, so that the colours very slightly spread until you have 4 concentric circles. Cook until the underside is bubbly then flip and cook for 30 seconds more. Repeat the process with the rest of the batter. Serve drizzled with chocolate sauce.

Pirate ship and treasure island cake

Prep:2 hrs and 30 mins **Cook:**45 mins

More effort

Serves 20 - 24

Ingredients

- 200g butter , cubed
- 300g dark plain chocolate , broken into pieces
- 200g plain flour
- ¾ tsp baking powder
- ¾ tsp bicarbonate of soda
- 250g light muscovado sugar , plus extra for decoration
- 3 eggs
- 200g soured cream
- 1 ½ tsp vanilla extract

For the icing and decoration

- 150g sieved apricot jam , warmed
- 650g brown ready-to-roll icing
- 18 mini Toblerones
- 6 malt chocolate balls

- 6 chocolate caramels (we used Rolos)
- 8 mini chocolate fingers
- 100g white marzipan
- gold covered chocolate coins
- chocolate skull (optional)
- 250g royal icing made from packet royal icing sugar (use 250g sugar)
- blue food colouring
- 1 chocolate stick (we used Mikado) (optional)

Equipment

- 30 x 20cm cake tin
- 30cm square cake board (preferably blue)
- 2 sheets black, white or blue paper
- 2 drinking straws
- 2 sandwich flags

Method

STEP 1

Heat the oven to 160C/140C fan/gas 3. Grease and line a 30x20cm cake tin with baking parchment.

STEP 2

Put the butter and 200g of the chocolate into a saucepan and heat gently until melted. Remove from the heat. Sieve the flour, baking powder and bicarbonate of soda into a large bowl. Mix in the sugar. Beat together the eggs, soured cream and vanilla extract. Pour the chocolate and egg mixtures into the flour and sugar and beat well until smooth. Pour into the prepared tin and bake in the oven for about 40 minutes. Leave until completely cold before cutting and shaping.

STEP 3

Cut the cake in half lengthways. Place one complete half on the 30cm cake board. Cut the remaining half into 3 rectangles, 13x10cm, 7x10cm and 10x10cm. Attach the 10x10cm piece to one end of the base cake using a little warm jam. Cut a 'V' shape to represent the prow of the ship. Place the 13x10 piece at the other end of the base cake, attaching with jam. Using jam again attach the 7x10 piece on top of the 13x10 piece to make the upper deck. Slice the back of the ship at a very slight angle.

STEP 4

Brush the whole cake with jam. Roll out about 550g of the ready-to-roll icing and cover the cake. Trim the edges at the base and keep any trimmings.

STEP 5

Melt the remaining 100g chocolate in the microwave or in a heatproof bowl over a saucepan of barely simmering water. Use melted chocolate to stick the mini Toblerones to the edges of the two decks and to the 'V' shape of the prow. Trim any to fit exactly. Use the chocolate to stick on the chocolate balls for canon balls, finger biscuits stacked up as canons and chocolate caramels for port holes. Using a little of the marzipan, roll out and cut four windows. Make window frames from brown icing trimmings, rolling out to thin sausages to form a cross and sticking with chocolate. Attach to the sides of the ship with chocolate. Poke the chocolate stick out of the front of the prow, if using.

STEP 6

Arrange the chocolate coins in a little pile on the cake board, reserving 3 or 4 coins for the top. Roll out the remaining brown icing and cover the coins completely. Brush with melted chocolate and sprinkle with muscovado sugar. Push 3 or 4 coins into the sand along with the chocolate skull if using.

STEP 7

Put a little of the royal icing in a bowl. Colour the remainder blue. Spread the icing on the cake board around the ship and the island. Use the white icing to make 'surf' around the edge of the island.

STEP 8

Using the remaining marzipan and brown icing, make three barrels. Place one on the deck of the ship and the others in the sea. Cut out sails from the paper and make holes in them so you can push the straws through. Attach the sails to the ship and poke sandwich flags out of the top to finish.

Sweet sushi

Prep:40 mins **Cook:**5 mins

plus setting

Easy

Makes 24

Ingredients

- 45g butter
- 280g marshmallows
- 340g Rice Krispies

To decorate

- 10 cola belts
- 50g dark or milk chocolate , melted
- 50g millions
- 50g apricot jam
- 2 red pencil sweets
- 2 green pencil sweets
- 100g ready-to-roll fondant icing
- orange, red and purple food colouring
- white and green food colouring powder
- 25g black treacle

Method

STEP 1

To make your bases melt the butter and marshmallows in a large saucepan. Once melted, gently stir in the Rice Krispies. Pour the mixture onto a lined 30cm x 20cm tray and press down firmly to compact the Rice Krispies and make flat. Leave to set for 1-2 hours.

STEP 2

Once set, cut out 12 small circles with a small round cutter using a small sharp knife to cut all the way through to the bottom if needed. Use the rest of the mix to make 10 rectangular pieces.

STEP 3

Cut your cola belts to size, measuring them around the cutter. Stick them with a small smudge of melted chocolate. Repeat on all 10 and leave to set. Mix the millions and jam together and put small heaps on 6 of the circles to look like caviar. On the remaining 6 pieces, get a chopstick and make 4 indents in the centre of the rice. Cut your pencil sweets into small pieces and poke them into the indents alternating in colour.

STEP 4

To decorate the rectangles, split your fondant icing in half and colour half orange and half a purple/red colour so they look like salmon and tuna. Roll each out to 5mm thick. Use a knife to cut out shapes that will fit on top of the rectangles and use the back of a knife to make fine imprints to make the pieces more flesh-like. On the orange 'salmon' pieces, paint the imprints with the white colouring powder. Place all the bits of decorated icing on top of the rectangular bases, moulding them to look as natural as possible.

STEP 5

Use the green food colouring powder to brush the cola belts and create a seaweed effect.

STEP 6

Finally to make your 'soy sauce' heat the black treacle and 50ml water in a pan until combined. Brush over the 'tuna' and 'salmon' sushi pieces and put the rest in a bowl as a dipping sauce.

Marshmallows dipped in chocolate

Prep:10 mins **Cook:**5 mins

Plus setting time

Easy

Makes 26 approx

Ingredients

- 50g white chocolate
- 50g milk chocolate
- selection of cake sprinkles
- 1 bag marshmallows (about 200g)
- 1 pack lollipop sticks

Method

STEP 1

Heat the chocolate in separate bowls over simmering water or on a low setting in the microwave. Allow to cool a little.

STEP 2

Put your chosen sprinkles on separate plates. Push a cake pop or lolly stick into a marshmallow about half way in. Dip into the white or milk chocolate, allow the excess to drip off then dip into the sprinkles of your choice. Put into a tall glass to set. Repeat with each marshmallow.

Barbecued chicken fajita skewers

Prep:30 mins **Cook:**10 mins

Easy

Makes 6-8 skewers

Ingredients

For the fajitas

- 2 limes , plus wedges to serve
- 1 tsp dried oregano
- 1 tsp ground cumin
- 1 tsp smoked paprika
- 1 tsp olive oil
- 2 garlic cloves , crushed or finely grated
- 4 chicken breasts
- 3 mixed coloured peppers
- 1 red onion

For the guacamole

- 2 ripe avocados
- 1 lime
- 6 cherry tomatoes , halved
- warmed tortillas , chopped coriander, soured cream or yogurt, plus chilli sauce for the grown-ups, to serve

Method

STEP 1

Make the marinade. In a large bowl, juice both the limes. Add the oregano, spices, olive oil and garlic, and mix together. Dice the chicken, then get your child to stir it through the marinade, and set aside.

STEP 2

Prepare the vegetables. Deseeding the peppers and halving the onion is tricky, so do this yourself. Children aged from about seven or above can cut them into chunks using a child-friendly knife.

STEP 3

Make your skewers. Carefully thread alternate pieces of chicken, peppers and onion onto your skewers. Smaller children might find this a little hard, so the best way is to stab the ingredients and push them up the skewers. When you've used up all the ingredients, set aside. Can be made several hours ahead and chilled until ready to cook.

STEP 4

Prepare the guacamole. Stone and peel the avocados, then tip into a bowl with the other ingredients. Get your child to use a potato masher to mash everything together and tip into a serving dish.

STEP 5

Cook the skewers. Heat a barbecue or griddle pan. Cook the skewers for 10-12 mins, turning, until they are cooked all the way through. A child from the age of eight can watch over a griddle and turn the skewers with a pair of tongs. Serve the skewers on heated tortillas with the guacamole, soured cream, chopped coriander, lime wedges on the side and chilli sauce for those who like a touch of spice.

Happy lion birthday cake

Prep:20 mins **Cook:**25 mins

plus cooling and decorating

Easy

Serves 16-18 or more if cut into rectangles

Ingredients

- 250g pack unsalted butter
- 50ml whole milk
- 150g whole natural yogurt
- ½ tsp vanilla paste or extract
- 3 large eggs
- 250g white caster sugar
- 300g self-raising flour

- 2 tsp baking powder

To fill and cover

- 200g unsalted butter , very well softened
- 300g icing sugar
- 1 tsp vanilla paste or extract
- 2 tsp whole milk
- 2 heaped tbsp raspberry jam (or lemon curd)

To decorate the cake

- 25cm cake board , or cake plate
- yellow or orange food colouring paste (we used Sugarflair Egg Yellow)
- about 350g white sugar paste
- a few strands of spaghetti , snipped into finger lengths
- a little icing sugar , sifted, for rolling out
- 2 liquorice Catherine wheels with blue middles
- about 2 tsp chocolate sprinkles

Method

STEP 1

Heat the oven to 180C/fan 160C/gas 4. Use a little of the butter to grease the sides and bases of two 20cm sandwich tins. Melt the rest of the butter in a small saucepan. Off the heat, add the milk, yogurt and vanilla, followed by the eggs. Beat well with a fork.

STEP 2

Put the dry ingredients plus ¼ tsp salt into a large bowl. Whisk to combine – this aerates and saves sifting. Tip in the wet ingredients and whisk to a smooth, silky batter.

STEP 3

Don't hang around at this point. Pour the batter evenly into the prepared tins and put onto the middle shelf in the oven. Bake for 25 mins or until risen and a skewer inserted into the middle of the cakes comes out clean. Cool for 10 mins in the tins, then carefully invert the cakes and leave to cool upside down on a cooling rack.

STEP 4

Make the buttercream. Put the butter into a large bowl and sift the icing sugar on top. Add the vanilla and milk and a pinch of salt then beat for a few mins with electric beaters until creamy, pale and spreadable.

STEP 5

Place one of the cakes onto the board or plate, and use a dab of buttercream underneath the cake to stop it slipping about. Spread with 1/4 of the buttercream and then all of the jam, if using.

STEP 6

Sandwich the second cake on top. Set aside 1 tsp buttercream to affix the ears later, then mound the rest on top of the cake. Use a palette knife to paddle it evenly over and down the sides. Set aside.

STEP 7

For the lion's mane and cheeks, use a little of the colouring paste to colour the sugarpaste yellow or orange, then split the paste in half. Add more colouring paste to one half and knead again to make it a shade darker. Roll two walnut-size balls of the darker paste to make the cheeks. Poke in the spaghetti to make whiskers, then set aside.

STEP 8

Using a little icing sugar, roll out the rest to about 2 x £1 coin thickness then cut into 12 squares measuring about 4 x 4cm. Re-roll any trimmings. Shape two small blobs into ears.

STEP 9

Position the squares around the cake, alternating lighter and darker yellow. Let the squares overhang the cake slightly with only the innermost corners meeting. Scatter the chocolate sprinkles into the gaps in-between.

STEP 10

Unroll a Catherine wheel. Cut two lengths of 20cm. Loop one end of each piece, then position on the cake to make the eyes and sides of the lion's nose. Poke into the buttercream. Add another strip of liquorice down the centre of the nose and a wiggly line to one side to give it some shadowing, if you like.

STEP 11

Make the bottom of the nose by snipping ever-decreasing lengths of liquorice and poking them into the buttercream.

STEP 12

Add two more curls for his mouth and two for eyebrows. Position the round cheeks to the sides.

Put the middles of the Catherine wheels towards the bottom of the eyes to make pupils.

STEP 13

Put the cheeks onto the lion's face. Fix the ears on top using a small blob of leftover buttercream. Leave the cake to set for an hour before cutting. If the sponges are used fresh or within a day of baking (wrap well once cooled), the finished cake will keep in a cool place (not the fridge) for 3 days.

Winter wonderland cake

Prep:1 hr **Cook:**35 mins

Plus cooling

Easy

Serves 12

Ingredients

- 175g unsalted butter , softened, plus more for the tin
- 250g golden caster sugar
- 3 large eggs
- 225g plain flour
- 2 tsp baking powder
- 50g crème fraîche
- 100g dark chocolate , melted and cooled a little
- 3 tbsp strawberry jam
- 8-10 candy canes , red and white
- mini white meringues and jelly sweets, to decorate

For the angel frosting

- 500g white caster sugar
- 1 tsp vanilla extract
- 1 tbsp liquid glucose
- 2 egg whites
- 30g icing sugar , sifted

Method

STEP 1

Heat oven to 180C/160C fan/gas 4. Butter and line three 18cm (or two 20cm) cake tins. Beat the butter and sugar together until light and fluffy. Add the eggs, beating them in one at a time. Fold in the flour, baking powder and a pinch of salt, then fold in the crème fraîche and chocolate and 100ml boiling water.

STEP 2

Divide the cake mixture between the tins and level the tops of the batter. Bake for 25-30 mins or until a skewer inserted into the middle comes out clean. Leave to cool for 10 mins in the tin, then tip out onto a cooling rack and peel off the parchment. Set aside to cool completely.

STEP 3

To make the angel frosting, put the sugar, vanilla and liquid glucose in a pan with 125ml water. Bring to the boil and cook until the sugar has melted – the syrup turns clear and the mixture hits 130C on a sugar thermometer (be very careful with hot sugar). Take off the heat. Meanwhile, beat the egg whites until stiff then, while still beating, gradually pour in the hot sugar syrup in a steady stream. Keep beating until the mixture is fluffy and thick enough to spread – this might take a few mins as the mixture cools. Beat in the icing sugar.

STEP 4

Spread two of the sponges with jam and some of the icing mixture, then sandwich the cakes together with the plain one on top. Use a little of the frosting to ice the whole cake (don't worry about crumbs at this stage). Use the remaining icing to ice the cake again, smoothing the side, and swirling it on top. Crush four of the candy canes and sprinkle over the cake, then add the remaining whole candy canes, meringues and sweets.

Bacon bolognese

Prep:10 mins **Cook:**12 mins

Easy

Serves 4

Ingredients

- 400g spaghetti
- 1 tsp olive oil
- 2 large carrots , finely diced

- 3 celery sticks, finely diced
- 200g pack smoked bacon lardon
- 190g jar sundried tomato pesto
- 8-12 basil leaves , shredded (optional)

Method

STEP 1

Boil the spaghetti following pack instructions. Meanwhile, heat the oil in a non-stick pan. Add the carrots, celery and bacon, and stir well. Cover the pan and cook, stirring occasionally, for 10 mins until the veg has softened.

STEP 2

Tip in the pesto, warm through, then stir through the drained spaghetti with the basil, if using.

Nutty cinnamon & yogurt dipper

Prep:5 mins

No cook

Easy

Serves 1

Ingredients

- 100g natural Greek yogurt
- 1 tbsp nut butter (try almond or cashew)
- ¼ tsp ground cinnamon
- 1 tsp honey

To serve

- apple wedges (tossed in a little lemon juice to prevent them turning brown)
- celery sticks
- carrot sticks
- mini rice cakes or crackers (choose gluten-free brands if necessary)

Method

STEP 1

In a small tub, mix together the yogurt, nut butter, cinnamon and honey. Serve with apple wedges (tossed in a little lemon juice to prevent them turning brown), celery or carrot sticks, and mini rice cakes or crackers.

Vanilla chick biscuit pops

Prep:15 mins **Cook:**6 mins - 7 mins

plus chilling and cooling

Easy

Makes 15-18 biscuits

Ingredients

- 200g unsalted butter , at room temperature
- 100g golden caster sugar
- 1 medium egg , beaten
- 1 tsp vanilla extract
- 200g plain flour , plus extra for dusting
- 200g icing sugar
- 2 tbsp milk
- few drops yellow food colouring
- 75g unsweetened desiccated coconut
- 50g small chocolate chips
- 25g orange or white fondant icing , plus a few drops orange food colouring

You will need

- 15-18 lolly sticks (see tip)
- ribbon , to decorate (optional)

Method

STEP 1

Put half the butter and all the sugar in a bowl. Using an electric whisk or wooden spoon, beat together until smooth and creamy. Beat in the egg and half the vanilla extract until thoroughly combined.

STEP 2

Tip the flour into the mixture and mix on a low speed until it comes together to form a dough. Gather up into a ball, wrap in cling film and chill in the fridge for 20 mins.

STEP 3

Heat oven to 180C/160C fan/gas 4. Line 2 baking trays with baking parchment. Put the biscuit dough on a lightly floured surface and roll out until about 5mm thick. Cut out the biscuits using a 6cm round cutter. Transfer the biscuits to the prepared trays and insert the lolly sticks into the sides, just a quarter of the way through. Bake for 6-7 mins until the edges are golden brown, then carefully transfer to a wire rack and allow to cool completely before decorating.

STEP 4

Meanwhile, make some buttercream frosting. Place the remaining softened butter in a bowl and beat with a wooden spoon. Slowly add the icing sugar, 1 tbsp at a time, until thoroughly incorporated and you have a smooth, creamy mixture. Add a little milk and the remaining vanilla extract with a few drops of food colouring to give a pale yellow colour. Chill for 5 mins.

STEP 5

Put the desiccated coconut in a small bowl, add a few drops of yellow food colouring and mix well until the coconut is coloured pale yellow.

STEP 6

Spread the buttercream frosting over one side of the biscuit and sprinkle with the coconut. Add 2 chocolate chip eyes to each. Pinch a little orange fondant icing and shape into a beak and press into the mixture. Decorate with a ribbon, if you like, and serve. Will keep for 2 days in an airtight container.

Pressed picnic sandwich

Prep:25 mins **Cook:**3 mins

Easy

Serves 8

Ingredients

- long ciabatta loaf, sliced in half lengthways
- 3 tbsp olive oil
- 1 tbsp balsamic vinegar

- 2 garlic cloves , finely chopped
- 1 tsp Dijon mustard
- 2 big handfuls of baby spinach
- 8 marinated artichoke hearts from a jar, quartered
- 250g roasted red pepper from a jar
- 8 slices prosciutto
- big handful of basil
- 125g ball mozzarella , cut into slices
- ½ red onion , very finely sliced

Method

STEP 1

Ask an adult to slice the ciabatta loaf in half lengthways and heat the oven to 200C/180C fan/gas 6.

STEP 2

Put the ciabatta loaf halves, crust-side down, on a large baking tray and drizzle with a little olive oil. Pop them in the oven for a few mins until just golden and lightly toasted.

STEP 3

Put the olive oil, balsamic vinegar, garlic and mustard in a bowl, then whisk them together with a fork.

STEP 4

Remove the toasted ciabatta halves from the tray and drizzle the bottom slice with about half of the dressing.

STEP 5

Arrange the rest of the ingredients in layers. Start with a large handful of baby spinach, then a few artichoke hearts.

STEP 6

Next add the slices of pepper, the prosciutto, basil, mozzarella and, finally, the red onion.

STEP 7

Drizzle over the rest of the dressing and pop the other slice of ciabatta on top.

STEP 8

Press down on the sandwich to squash all the layers together.

STEP 9

Wrap the sandwich in baking parchment and tie it together with a couple of pieces of string.

STEP 10

Place a heavy baking tray on top of your sandwich and top it with weights or loaf tins filled with baking beans. Pop it all in the fridge overnight or until you are ready to eat it. Cut and serve in slices for the perfect picnic snack.

RECIPE TIPS

EQUIPMENT YOU WILL NEED

Chopping board, knife, 2 baking trays, oven gloves, small bowl, fork, spoon, baking parchment, ball of string, weights or loaf tins filled with baking beans.

ADAPTING FLAVOURS

If your kids aren't keen on some of the flavours, simply swap them for fillings they do like. Try, for example, ham, cheddar & tomato or tuna, watercress & cucumber.

Christmas pudding Rice Krispie cakes

Prep:30 hrs **Cook:**5 mins

plus chilling

Easy

Makes 10 - 12

Ingredients

- 50g rice pops (we used Rice Krispies)
- 30g raisin , chopped
- 50g butter
- 100g milk chocolate , broken into pieces
- 2 tbsp crunchy peanut butter
- 30g mini marshmallow
- 80g white chocolate

- ready-made icing holly leaves (we used Sainsbury's Christmas cake decorations)

Method

STEP 1

Put the rice pops and raisins into a bowl. Put the butter, milk chocolate, peanut butter and marshmallows into a small saucepan. Place on a medium to low heat and stir until the chocolate and butter have melted but the marshmallows are just beginning to melt.

STEP 2

Pour onto the rice pops and stir until well coated. Line an egg cup with cling film. Press about a tablespoon of the mixture into the egg cup. Press firmly and then remove, peel off the cling film and place the pudding into a cake case, flat-side down. Repeat with the remaining mixture. Chill until firm.

STEP 3

Melt the white chocolate in the microwave or in bowl over a saucepan of barely simmering water. Spoon a little chocolate over the top of each pudding. Top with icing holly leaves.

Whisky & pink peppercorn marmalade kit

Easy

Ingredients

- 500g mix of oranges , clementines and lemons
- 1kg demerara sugar
- small pot of pink peppercorns
- small bottle of whisky

Optional extras

- jam pan
- muslin
- large wooden spoon
- small jars and labels (makes about 1kg jam)

To use kit

see tip

Method

STEP 1

To use the kit: *Write the following instructions on the gift tag:*
Halve the fruits and squeeze the juices into a large saucepan. Remove all the peel and set aside.
Put the flesh in the pan with 1 litre water and boil for 15 mins. Push through a sieve lined with
muslin and return the liquid to the pan.

STEP 2

Shred the peel and tip into a heatproof bowl. Add enough water to just cover and microwave for
3-4 mins until soft. Add the peel to the pan, then add the sugar. Boil for 35-45 mins until the
marmalade has reached setting point (keep an eye on it so it doesn't bubble over).

STEP 3

Remove from the heat and add 1 tsp pink peppercorns. Allow the mixture to cool a little, then
stir in 50ml whisky. Ladle into sterilised jars and seal. Will keep for up to one year.

Yummy chocolate log

Prep:30 mins **Cook:**10 mins

More effort

Serves 8

Ingredients

For the cake

- 3 eggs
- 85g golden caster sugar
- 85g plain flour (minus 2 tbsp)
- 2 tbsp cocoa powder
- ½ tsp baking powder

For the filling & icing

- 50g butter, plus extra for the tin
- 140g dark chocolate , broken into squares
- 1 tbsp golden syrup
- 284ml pot double cream

- 200g icing sugar, sifted
- 2-3 extra strong mints, crushed (optional)
- icing sugar and holly sprigs to decorate - ensure you remove the berries before serving

Method

STEP 1

Heat the oven to 200C/180C fan/gas 6. Butter and line a 23 x 32cm Swiss roll tin with baking parchment. Beat the eggs and golden caster sugar together with an electric whisk for about 8 mins until thick and creamy.

STEP 2

Mix the flour, cocoa powder and baking powder together, then sift onto the egg mixture. Fold in very carefully, then pour into the tin. Tip the tin from side to side to spread the mixture into the corners. Bake for 10 mins.

STEP 3

Lay a sheet of baking parchment on a work surface. When the cake is ready, tip it onto the parchment, peel off the lining paper, then roll the cake up from its longest edge with the paper inside. Leave to cool.

STEP 4

To make the icing, melt the butter and dark chocolate together in a bowl over a pan of hot water. Take from the heat and stir in the golden syrup and 5 tbsp double cream. Beat in the icing sugar until smooth.

STEP 5

Whisk the remaining double cream until it holds its shape. Unravel the cake, spread the cream over the top, scatter over the crushed extra strong mints, if using, then carefully roll up again into a log.

STEP 6

Cut a thick diagonal slice from one end of the log. Lift the log on to a plate, then arrange the slice on the side with the diagonal cut against the cake to make a branch. Spread the icing over the log and branch (don't cover the ends), then use a fork to mark the icing to give the effect of tree bark. Scatter with unsifted icing sugar to resemble snow, and decorate with holly.

Pudsey bear cake

Prep:1 hr and 15 mins **Cook:**30 mins

Easy

Serves 10 - 12

Ingredients

- 225g softened butter
- 225g golden caster sugar
- 4 large eggs
- ½ lemon , zested
- 1 tsp vanilla extract
- 225g self-raising flour
- splash of milk

For the filling and covering

- 200g icing sugar
- 100g butter , softened
- 2 tsp milk
- 50g raspberry jam or strawberry jam, plus extra for sticking
- icing sugar for dusting
- 250g white fondant

To decorate

- 200g black sugar paste
- 100g yellow sugar paste
- 25g white fondant
- red, green and blue, fondant or coloured icing pens

Method

STEP 1

Heat oven to 180C/160C fan/gas 4, butter and line the base of two 20cm spring-form cake tins with baking parchment.

STEP 2

Using an electric whisk, beat the butter and sugar together until pale and fluffy. Crack the eggs in one at a time and whisk well, scraping down the sides of the bowl after each addition. Add the lemon zest, vanilla, flour, milk and a pinch of salt. Whisk until just combined then divide the mixture between the two tins.

STEP 3

Bake in the centre of the oven for 25-30 mins until a skewer inserted into the middle of each cake comes out clean. After 10 mins remove the cakes from their tins and leave to cool completely on a wire rack.

STEP 4

While the cakes cool, stir together the icing sugar, butter and milk for the filling. Once roughly mixed switch to using electric beaters until smooth and pale. When the cake is cold spread one third of the buttercream over one of the sponges and top with the jam. Smooth it over evenly then top with the other sponge. Spread the buttercream all over the outside of the sandwiched cake in an even thin layer and chill in the fridge until needed.

STEP 5

Dust your work surface with icing sugar and roll out 250g white fondant so that it is big enough to cover the cake. Lay it over the chilled cake, smooth down the surface and trim off any excess. Now roll out the black sugar paste so it's approx. 5mm thick then cut into the shape of Pudsey's head (it's easier to do this if you draw a template first then draw around it). Use a little buttercream or water to stick this on top of the cake. Roll out the yellow sugar paste and cut a slightly smaller version of Pudsey's head to stick on top in the same way so that the black sugar paste becomes the outline.

STEP 6

Roll out the remaining fondant to make the eyepatch, nose, mouth and eye and eyebrow and stick all the pieces on with a little bit of water. Use coloured sugar paste or writing icing to create polka dots on the eye patch. Use a clean paintbrush dipped in water to remove any excess icing sugar from your design. Will keep covered for 2-3 days in a cool place.

Spicy meatballs

Prep:15 mins **Cook:**25 mins

Easy

Serves 6

Ingredients

* 500g minced chicken , turkey, lamb, beef or pork
* 1 medium onion
* 2 garlic cloves , crushed or chopped
* 2 tsp mild or medium curry powder
* 2 tsp ground cumin
* 1 tsp garam masala
* ½ tsp paprika or cayenne pepper
* 2 tbsp fresh coriander , chopped
* 1 egg , beaten
* 50g fresh breadcrumb
* 1 tbsp olive oil

Method

STEP 1

Heat oven to 180C/fan 160C/gas 4.

STEP 2

Put the mince into the mixing bowl. Add the onions, garlic, curry powder, cumin, garam masala, paprika or cayenne pepper and coriander, then mix well. By adding these spices, you'll get a delicious flavour without having to add any salt.

STEP 3

Add the beaten egg and breadcrumbs, then mix again.

STEP 4

Divide the meat mixture into 15-18 evensized pieces and shape into balls (they should be about the size of a walnut). Always wash your hands thoroughly after handling raw meat so you don't transfer any germs that may be on the meat to other food or equipment.

STEP 5

Heat the oil in the frying pan over a medium heat and add the meatballs using a spoon. Cook them for 5 mins, turning until golden brown. Remove from the pan and place them on to the tray. Bake in the oven for 15-20 mins.

STEP 6

Remove from the oven. Remember to use oven gloves! Allow to cool slightly and serve with a fresh, crisp green salad, some pitta bread and tomato salsa.

RECIPE TIPS

MAKE IT SAUCY

Fry 2 sliced garlic cloves in a little olive oil and add a 400g tin of chopped tomatoes. Bring to the boil, then transfer to an ovenproof dish. Add your meatballs, cover them with sauce and bake in the oven for 40 mins-1 hr. Serve with rice or pasta.

Sweet snowballs

Prep:20 mins **Cook:**5 mins

Plus chilling

Easy

Makes 16

Ingredients

- 400g white chocolate , broken into pieces
- 100g rich tea biscuit
- 50g white Malteser
- 50g mini marshmallow
- 50g dried cranberries
- 50g cake crumbs (we used shop-bought Madeira cake)
- 3 tbsp golden syrup
- 100g desiccated coconut
- edible glitter (optional)

Method

STEP 1

Melt the chocolate in a bowl over a pan of simmering water. Meanwhile, crush the biscuits and Maltesers in a large bowl with a rolling pin.

STEP 2

Add mini marshmallows, dried cranberries and cake crumbs, then the chocolate and golden syrup. Mix well. Tip desiccated coconut onto a plate. Drop large spoonfuls of mixture onto the plate, then roll them around, coating in coconut and shaping into balls. Place on a baking tray and chill for 30 mins before serving. Sprinkle with edible glitter if you like.

Vietnamese veggie hotpot

Prep:5 mins **Cook:**20 mins

Easy

Serves 4

Ingredients

- 2 tsp vegetable oil
- thumb-size piece fresh root ginger , shredded
- 2 garlic cloves , chopped
- ½ large butternut squash , peeled and cut into chunks
- 2 tsp soy sauce
- 2 tsp soft brown sugar
- 200ml vegetable stock
- 100g green bean , trimmed and sliced
- 4 spring onions , sliced
- coriander leaves and cooked basmati or jasmine rice, to serve

Method

STEP 1

Heat the oil in a medium-size, lidded saucepan. Add the ginger and garlic, then stir-fry for about 5 mins. Add the squash, soy sauce, sugar and stock. Cover, then simmer for 10 mins. Remove the lid, add the green beans, then cook for 3 mins more until the squash and beans are tender. Stir the spring onions through at the last minute, then sprinkle with coriander and serve with rice.

RECIPE TIPS

TRY IT WITH CHICKEN

Add 2 chicken breasts, sliced, to the ginger and garlic, then stir-fry for a few mins until browned. Stir in the squash, soy sauce, sugar, stock and 2 tbsp crunchy peanut butter, then cook as above. Remove the lid, cook for a few mins more until thickened, then scatter with coriander and serve spooned over bowls of rice.

Quick pitta pizzas

Prep:10 mins **Cook:**10 mins

Easy

Serves 2

Ingredients

- 4 wholewheat pitta breads
- 4 tsp sun-dried tomato purée
- 3 ripe plum tomatoes , diced
- 1 shallot , thinly sliced
- 85g chorizo , diced
- 50g mature cheddar , grated
- few basil leaves , if you like

Method

STEP 1

Heat oven to 200C/180C fan/gas 6 and put a baking sheet inside to heat up. Spread each pitta with 1 tsp purée. Top with the tomatoes, shallot, chorizo and cheddar.

STEP 2

Place on the hot sheet and bake for 10 mins until the pittas are crisp, the cheese has melted and the chorizo has frazzled edges. Scatter with basil, if you like, and serve with a green salad.

RECIPE TIPS

CHORIZO

For the best results, use a whole piece of chorizo and cut it yourself, rather than buying pre-sliced chorizo.

SWEETCORN & HAM PITTA PIZZAS

Spread the pittas with 4 tsp pesto in place of the sun-dried tomato purée, and replace the shallot and chorizo with a handful sweetcorn kernels and shredded ham. Cook as before.

Baileys banana trifles

Prep:10 mins

Easy

Serves 6

Ingredients

- 300g pot extra-thick double cream
- 7 tbsp Baileys
- 6 chocolate brownies (about 250g/9oz), broken up, or use crumbled chocolate biscuits or loaf cake
- 3 bananas , sliced
- 500g pot vanilla custard
- 6 tbsp toffee sauce
- 25g chocolate , grated

Method

STEP 1

Mix the cream with 1 tbsp Baileys, and set aside. Divide the brownie pieces between 6 glasses, then drizzle each with 1 tbsp Baileys. Top with the sliced bananas, custard and Baileys cream, dividing equally, then drizzle with toffee sauce and finish with grated chocolate. Can be made a few hours ahead.

Rainbow cookies

Prep:25 mins - 30 mins **Cook:**15 mins

Easy

Makes 22

Ingredients

- 175g softened butter
- 50g golden caster sugar
- 50g icing sugar
- 2 egg yolks
- 2 tsp vanilla extract
- 300g plain flour
- zest and juice 1 orange
- 140g icing sugar , sifted
- sprinkles , to decorate

Method

STEP 1

Heat oven to 200C/180C fan/gas 6. Mix the butter, sugars, egg yolks and vanilla with a wooden spoon until creamy, then mix in the flour in 2 batches. Stir in the orange zest. Roll the dough into about 22 walnut-size balls and sit on baking sheets. Bake for 15 mins until golden, then leave to cool.

STEP 2

Meanwhile, mix the icing sugar with enough orange juice to make a thick, runny icing. Dip each biscuit half into the icing, then straight into the sprinkles. Dry on a wire rack.

Christmas biscuits

Prep:40 mins **Cook:**15 mins

Plus chilling

Easy

Makes 30-40 depending on size

Ingredients

- 175g dark muscovado sugar
- 85g golden syrup
- 100g butter
- 3 tsp ground ginger
- 1 tsp ground cinnamon
- 350g plain flour, plus extra for dusting
- 1 tsp bicarbonate of soda
- 1 egg, lightly beaten

To finish

- 100g white chocolate
- edible silver balls

Method

STEP 1

Heat the sugar, golden syrup and butter until melted. Mix the spices and flour in a large bowl. Dissolve the bicarbonate of soda in 1 tsp cold water. Make a well in the centre of the dry ingredients, add the melted sugar mix, egg and bicarbonate of soda. Mix well. At this stage the mix will be soft but will firm up on cooling.

STEP 2

Cover the surface of the biscuit mix with wrapping and leave to cool, then put in the fridge for at least 1 hr to become firm enough to roll out.

STEP 3

Heat oven to 190C/170C fan/gas 5. Turn the dough out onto a lightly floured surface and knead briefly. (At this stage the dough can be put into a food bag and kept in the fridge for up to a week.) Cut the dough in half. Thinly roll out one half on a lightly floured surface. Cut into shapes with cutters, such as gifts, trees and hearts, then transfer to baking sheets, leaving a little room for them to spread. If you plan to hang the biscuits up, make a small hole in the top of each one using a skewer. Repeat with remaining dough.

STEP 4

Bake for 12-15 mins until they darken slightly. If the holes you have made have closed up, remake them while the biscuits are warm and soft using a skewer. Cool for a few mins on the baking sheets, then transfer to a wire rack to cool and harden up completely.

STEP 5

Break up the chocolate and melt in the microwave on Medium for 1-2 mins, or in a small heatproof bowl over simmering water. Drizzle the chocolate over the biscuits, or pipe on shapes or names, then stick a few silver balls into the chocolate. If hung up on the tree, the biscuits will be edible for about a week, but will last a lot longer as decorations.

Apple 'doughnuts'

Prep: 20 mins

No cook

Easy

Makes 15

Ingredients

- 150g soft cheese
- 2 tsp honey
- 3 apples (use a crunchy eating variety)
- 3-4 tbsp almond or peanut butter (optional)
- coloured sprinkles , to decorate

Method

STEP 1

Mix the soft cheese with the honey and set aside. Peel the apples, then slice each through the core into five or six rings, about 1cm thick. Use an apple corer or small round biscuit cutter to stamp out a circle from the middle of each slice, removing the core and creating 'doughnut' shapes. Pat the slices dry using kitchen paper – they should be as dry as possible to help the toppings stick.

STEP 2

Spread some nut butter over the slices, if using, then top with the sweetened soft cheese. Decorate with the sprinkles and serve.

Cheese roll-ups

Prep:30 mins **Cook:**25 mins

Easy

Makes 6

Ingredients

- 200g self-raising flour , plus extra for dusting
- 50g butter , softened
- 1 tsp paprika
- 100-125ml/3½-4fl oz milk
- 50g ready-grated mature cheddar

Method

STEP 1

Heat oven to 220C/200C fan/gas 7. Put the flour and butter in a bowl and rub them together with your fingers. Rubbing in mixture with cold butter is hard and tiring on young fingers, so use slightly softened butter – but not so soft that it is oily. Now stir in the paprika and mix again.

STEP 2

Add 100ml milk and mix with a fork until you get a soft dough. Add a splash more milk if the dough is dry. This process will teach you how to feel the dough and decide if it needs more liquid. You can always add more milk if required.

STEP 3

On a lightly floured surface, roll out the dough like pastry to about 0.5cm thick. Try to keep a rectangular shape. Only roll in one direction, and roll and turn, roll and turn – by keeping the dough moving, you avoid finding it stuck at the end.

STEP 4

Sprinkle the grated cheese on top, then roll up like a sausage along the long side. Cut into 12 thick rings using a table knife. Get an adult to show you how to hold the dough with one hand and cut straight through with the other.

STEP 5

Line the baking tray with baking parchment. Place the roll-ups on the parchment, cut-side down, almost touching each other, making sure that you can see the spiral. Get an adult to put them in the oven for you and bake for 20-25 mins until golden and melty. Ask an adult to remove them from the oven, then leave to cool. *The cheese roll-ups will keep for up to 3 days in an airtight container.*

Cuddly egg men

Prep:20 mins **Cook:**20 mins

Plus rising

Easy

Makes 4

Ingredients

- 400g strong white flour
- ½ tsp salt
- pinch of sugar
- 7g sachet fast-action dried yeast

- 2 tbsp olive oil
- 4 large eggs , at room temperature

Method

STEP 1

Put the flour into a large bowl and stir in the salt, sugar and yeast. Pour in 250ml water and the oil and mix to a soft dough. Add a little extra water if necessary.

STEP 2

Knead the dough for a few minutes until smooth and then put into a bowl, cover and leave in a warm place for about 1 hour or until doubled in size.

STEP 3

Heat the oven to 200C/180C fan/gas 6. Turn the dough out onto a board, knead briefly and then cut into four. Take one piece and cut off a quarter and shape into a ball for the head. Shape the other piece into a sausage. Attach the head to the body using a little cold water.

STEP 4

Place the dough onto a non-stick baking sheet. Using a sharp knife cut the bottom half of the sausage to make two legs, then cut into the sides up to the shoulders to make two arms. Using scissors, snip at intervals around the top of the head to make hair and make one snip for the mouth. Use a wooden skewer to make two eyes.

STEP 5

Take one egg and place on the dough man's tummy. Fold the arms over the egg and secure with a little cold water. Make three more egg men with the remaining dough. Leave to prove for about 10 mins.

STEP 6

Bake in the oven for 20 mins until well risen and golden. Cool on a wire rack for a few mins before peeling the egg and eating with the warm bread.

Fright Night fancies

Prep:25 mins

No cook

Easy

Serves 12

Ingredients

- 12 ready-made vanilla cupcakes or fairy cakes , or make your own (see tip)
- 2 x 410g cans apricot halves in light syrup, drained (reserve the syrup)
- 100g raspberry jam
- a little icing sugar or cornflour, for dusting
- 500g pack ready-to-roll white fondant icing
- black icing pen

Method

STEP 1

Remove the cakes from their paper cases – if the tops are rounded, trim them with a serrated knife to make a flat surface. Flip the cakes over and arrange on a large board or cake stand. Brush the cakes all over with the syrup from the drained apricots, then place 1 tsp jam on top of each cake. Put an apricot half on top of the jam, rounded- side facing up.

STEP 2

Clean your work surface, then dust with a little icing sugar or cornflour. Roll out the icing to the thickness of a 50p piece – it will be easier if you work with half at a time, keeping the remaining icing well wrapped so it doesn't dry out. Use a 12cm fluted cookie cutter to stamp out 12 circles and, as soon as you cut each one, drape it over a cake. Draw on spooky faces using the black icing pen, then serve. Can be made up to a day ahead; eat leftover cakes within 1 day.

RECIPE TIPS

ICING TIPS

Make sure you roll the icing out thickly enough, especially if you're not serving them immediately. If the icing is too thin it can become soggy when it touches the apricot. The ideal thickness would be the same as a 50p coin or around 2-3mm.

More veg, less meat summer Bolognese

Prep:15 mins **Cook:**40 mins

Easy

Serves 4

Ingredients

- 2 tbsp olive oil
- 2 onions , finely chopped
- 3 carrots , finely chopped
- 4 celery sticks, finely chopped
- 2 courgettes , cut into small cubes
- 4 garlic cloves , finely chopped
- 250g pack beef mince
- 1 heaped tbsp tomato purée
- 400g can chopped tomato
- 400g fettuccine
- 200g pea , frozen or fresh
- handful parsley , roughly chopped

Method

STEP 1

Heat the oil in large deep frying pan. Add the onions, carrots, celery, courgettes and garlic. Cook for about 10 mins or until soft, adding a few splashes of water if the mixture begins to stick. Turn up the heat and add the mince. Fry for a few mins more, breaking up the mince with the back of a spoon. Stir in tomato purée, pour over the chopped tomatoes and add a can of water. Simmer for 15 mins until the sauce is thick, then season.

STEP 2

Meanwhile, cook the fettuccine following pack instructions.

STEP 3

Tip the peas into the sauce and simmer for 2 mins more until tender. Stir through the drained pasta and parsley, then serve.

Courgette muffins

Prep:35 mins **Cook:**25 mins

Plus cooling

Easy

Makes 12

Ingredients

- 50g courgette , cut into chunks
- 1 apple , peeled and quartered
- 1 orange , halved
- 1 egg
- 75g butter , melted
- 300g self-raising flour
- ½ tsp baking powder
- ½ tsp cinnamon
- 100g golden caster sugar
- handful of sultanas
- 1 tub soft cheese mixed with 3 tbsp icing sugar, to make icing

Method

STEP 1

Brush the muffin tin with oil. **Ask your grown-up helper** to switch the oven to 190C/ 170C fan/gas 5.

STEP 2

Grate the courgettes and put them in a large bowl. Grate the apple and add to the bowl. Squeeze the orange and add the juice to the bowl.

STEP 3

Break the egg into a bowl; if any bits of shell get in, scoop them out with a spoon. Stir the butter and egg into the courgette and apple mix.

STEP 4

Sieve the flour, baking powder and cinnamon into the bowl. Add the sugar and sultanas.

STEP 5

Mix with a spoon until everything is combined, but don't worry if it is lumpy.

STEP 6

Spoon the mixture into the tin. **Ask your helper** to put it in the oven and cook for 20-25 mins. Cool in the tin, then spread some icing on each.

Rainbow fruit skewers

Prep: 15 mins

Serves 7

Ingredients

- 7 raspberries
- 7 hulled strawberries
- 7 tangerine segments
- 7 cubes peeled mango
- 7 peeled pineapple chunks
- 7 peeled kiwi fruit chunks
- 7 green grapes
- 7 red grapes
- 14 blueberries

Method

STEP 1

Take 7 wooden skewers and thread the following fruit onto each – 1 raspberry, 1 hulled strawberry, 1 tangerine segment, 1 cube of peeled mango, 1 chunk of peeled pineapple, 1 chunk of peeled kiwi, 1 green and 1 red grape, and finish off with 2 blueberries. Arrange in a rainbow shape and let everyone help themselves.

Pepper & walnut hummus with veggie dippers

Prep: 10 mins **Cook:** 6 mins

Serves 2

Ingredients

- 400g can chickpeas , drained
- 1 garlic clove
- 1 large roasted red pepper from a jar (not in oil), about 100g
- 1 tbsp tahini paste
- juice ½ lemon
- 4 walnut halves , chopped
- 2 courgettes , cut into batons

- 2 carrots , cut into batons
- 2 celery sticks, cut into batons

Method

STEP 1

Put the chickpeas, garlic, pepper, tahini and lemon juice in a bowl. Blitz with a hand blender or in a food processor to make a thick purée. Stir in the walnuts. Pack into pots, if you like, and serve with the veggie sticks. Will keep in the fridge for two days, although the vegetables are best prepared fresh to preserve their vitamins.

Fruit & nut yogurt

Prep:5 mins **Cook:**5 mins

Serves 1

Ingredients

- 3 tbsp chopped mixed nut
- 1 tbsp sunflower seed
- 1 tbsp pumpkin seed
- 1 sliced banana
- 1-2 handfuls berries (frozen and defrosted is fine)
- 200g vanilla yogurt

Method

STEP 1

Mix the nuts, sunflower seeds and pumpkin seeds. Mix the sliced banana and berries. Layer up in a bowl with yoghurt and enjoy.

Turkey & pepper pittas

Prep:15 mins **Cook:**12 mins

Serves 2

Ingredients

- 1 tbsp olive oil
- 200g turkey breast steak , cut into strips
- pinch chilli flakes

- 1 red and 1 yellow pepper , deseeded and cut into strips
- 3 spring onions , trimmed and sliced
- 1 avocado , stoned, peeled and sliced
- handful coriander leaves
- 2 wholemeal pitta breads , toasted and halved to form pockets
- 2 tbsp soured cream

Method

STEP 1

Heat the oil in a wok or large frying pan and fry the turkey and chilli flakes for 5-6 mins. Add the peppers and spring onions and stir-fry until the turkey is cooked but the peppers still have crunch. Season.

STEP 2

Divide the avocado and coriander between the pitta halves, then spoon in the turkey and pepper mix. Add a dollop of soured cream to each and serve straight away.

Instant frozen berry yogurt

Prep:2 mins

Serves 4

Ingredients

- 250g frozen mixed berry
- 250g 0%-fat Greek yogurt
- 1 tbsp honey or agave syrup

Method

STEP 1

Blend berries, yogurt and honey or agave syrup in a food processor for 20 seconds, until it comes together to a smooth ice-cream texture. Scoop into bowls and serve.

Healthier flapjacks

Prep:10 mins **Cook:**20 mins

Makes 12

Ingredients

- 150g ready-to-eat stoned dates
- 100g low-fat spread
- 3 generous tbsp agave syrup
- 50g ready-to-eat stoned dried apricots, finely chopped
- 50g chopped toasted hazelnuts
- 3 tbsp mixed seeds
- 50g raisins
- 150g porridge oats

Method

STEP 1

Heat the oven to 190C/170C fan/gas 5. Line an 18cm square tin with baking parchment. Put the dates into a food processor and blitz until they are finely chopped and sticking together in clumps.

STEP 2

Put the low-fat spread, agave syrup and dates into a saucepan and heat gently. Stir until the low-fat spread has melted and the dates are blended in. Add all the remaining ingredients to the pan and stir until well mixed. Spoon the mixture into the tin and spread level.

STEP 3

Bake in the oven for 15-20 mins until golden brown. Remove and cut into 12 pieces. Leave in the tin until cold. Store in an airtight container.

Lemon & coriander hummus

Prep:5 mins

Serves 6

Ingredients

- 2 x cans chickpeas in water, drained
- 2 fat garlic cloves , roughly chopped
- 3 tbsp Greek yogurt
- 3 tbsp tahini paste
- 3 tbsp extra-virgin olive oil , plus extra
- zest and juice 2 lemons
- 20g pack coriander

Method

STEP 1

Put everything but the coriander into a food processor, then whizz to a fairly smooth mix. Scrape down the sides of the processor if you need to.

STEP 2

Season the hummus generously, then add the coriander and pulse until roughly chopped. Spoon into a serving bowl, drizzle with olive oil, then serve.

Mango & banana smoothie

Prep:5 mins

Makes 1 litre

Ingredients

- 1 medium mango
- 1 banana
- 500ml orange juice
- 4 ice cubes

Method

STEP 1

Cut the mango down either side of the flat stone, then peel and cut the flesh into chunks.

STEP 2

Peel and chop the banana.

STEP 3

Put all the ingredients into a food processor or blender, then process until smooth and thick. Keep in the fridge and use the day you make it.

Peach Melba smoothie

Prep:5 mins

Serves 2

Ingredients

- 410g can peach halves

- 100g frozen raspberry , plus a few for garnish
- 100ml orange juice
- 150ml fresh custard , plus a spoonful for garnish

Method

STEP 1

Drain and rinse peaches and place in a blender with raspberries. Add orange juice and fresh custard and whizz together.

STEP 2

Pour over ice, garnish with another spoonful of custard and a few raspberries. Best served chilled.

Spiced apple crisps

Prep:5 mins Cook:1 hr

Serves 1

Ingredients

- 2 Granny Smiths
- cinnamon , for sprinkling

Method

STEP 1

Heat the oven to 160C/ 140C fan/ gas mark 3. Core the apple and slice through the equator into very thin slices 1 - 2mm thick. Dust with cinnamon and lay flat on a baking sheet lined with parchment paper.

STEP 2

Cook for 45 mins – 1 hour, turning halfway through and removing any crisps that have turned brown. Continue cooking until the apples have dried out and are light golden. Cool, store in an airtight container and enjoy as a snack.

Sweet & spicy popcorn

Prep:5 mins **Cook:**2 mins

Serves 2

Ingredients

- 100g bag salted microwave popcorn
- ¼ tsp chilli powder
- ½ tsp cinnamon
- 1 tbsp agave syrup

Method

STEP 1

Cook the microwave popcorn according to the packet instructions. Tip into a large bowl. Sprinkle over the spices, then pour over the agave syrup. Stir and serve warm or pour into a bag and take to work as an afternoon snack.

Turkey & avocado toast

Prep:10 mins **Cook:**5 mins

Serves 2

Ingredients

- 1 avocado
- juice ½ lime
- 2-3 small slices ciabatta bread
- 100g turkey slices

Method

STEP 1

Halve and stone the avocado then scrape out the flesh into a bowl. Squeeze in the lime, season, then mash roughly with a fork. Toast the ciabatta, spread with mashed avocado, top with turkey and finish with ground black pepper.

Almond butter

Prep:15 mins **Cook:**10 mins

Makes a 300g jar

Ingredients

- 300g skin-on almond
- good drizzle honey
- malt loaf or wholegrain bread, to serve (optional)

Method

STEP 1

Heat oven to 190C/170C fan/gas 5. Spread the almonds on a baking tray and roast for 10 mins. Remove and allow to cool.

STEP 2

Put into a food processor and whizz for 12 mins, stopping every so often to scrape the sides down, and finish with a drizzle of honey. Serve spread over malt loaf or wholegrain bread. *Will keep in the fridge for up to 3 weeks.*

Frozen fruit sticks with passion fruit & lime drizzle

Prep:20 mins

Makes 8

Ingredients

- 100g strawberries , hulled and halved
- 8 seedless grapes
- 100g/4oz mango chunks
- 100g/4oz melon chunks
- 2 kiwi fruit , peeled and cut into chunks
- 100g/4oz pineapple chunks

For the drizzle

- juice 2 limes
- 4 passion fruits , halved and seeds scraped out
- 1 tsp icing sugar

Method

STEP 1

Mix the drizzle ingredients in a small bowl, stirring until the sugar has dissolved. If you want the sauce to be smooth, pass it through a sieve to remove the seeds, or leave them in if you prefer.

STEP 2

Skewer the fruits onto wooden skewers and drizzle the sauce on top, reserving a little for dipping. Pop the skewers in the freezer for 45 mins, until just starting to freeze. Serve with the leftover drizzle.

Wrap-your-own spring rolls

Prep:40 mins **Cook:**25 mins

Makes 8 - 10

Ingredients

- 300g pack cooked rice noodles from the chiller cabinet (see tips)
- about 400g/14oz mixed vegetables , thinly sliced and put in separate bowls, such as red peppers, beansprouts, carrots, shredded Chinese leaf cabbage, spring onions
- 140g cooked prawns
- 100g cooked chicken or duck, shredded
- 2 garlic cloves , finely chopped
- small piece ginger , finely chopped
- splash light soy sauce
- Chinese five-spice powder , for sprinkling
- 8-10 sheets of brik or filo pastry (see tips)
- 1 egg , beaten
- sesame seeds , for sprinkling if you want

For the dipping sauce

- 100g reduced salt and sugar ketchup
- 1 tbsp white wine vinegar
- small piece ginger , grated
- pinch of caster sugar

Method

STEP 1

Heat oven to 200C/180C fan/gas 6. Before you get the kids cooking, put the noodles, vegetables, prawns and chicken in individual bowls for everyone to help themselves. Wash hands, put aprons on, sit the kids down and give them their own mixing bowl and spoon. Let them choose which ingredients they want (noodles are essential) in their rolls and if they want to graze as they choose, that's fine – all the ingredients are cooked or can be eaten raw. Add a bit of garlic and ginger, a tiny dash of soy and sprinkling of five-spice to each bowl and let them mix everything together.

STEP 2

Push the bowl aside and lay a sheet of pastry in front of each child. Ask them to spoon the filling down one side of each sheet then give them the beaten egg and a brush so they can brush around the edges. Then help them to roll them up neatly by folding both sides over the filling, then rolling them up.

STEP 3

Lift the spring rolls onto a baking tray, seam side down, brush with a little more egg and sprinkle with sesame seeds, if you want. Try to remember which child made which roll to save any arguments at the end! Bake the rolls for 20-25 mins or until golden.

STEP 4

While the rolls are in the oven, make the dipping sauce. Get the kids to mix all the ingredients together until the sugar has dissolved. When the spring rolls are golden and crisp, remove from the oven. Leave until cool enough to handle, cut into pieces for smaller kids, then let them eat, dipping the rolls into the sauce.

Apple crunch

Prep:1 min

Serves 1

Ingredients

- 1 small eating apple
- 1 tbsp organic unsalted crunchy peanut butter

Method

STEP 1

Cut the apple in half and spread with the peanut butter.

Banana, honey & hazelnut smoothie

Prep:5 mins

Serves 2

Ingredients

- 1 peeled, sliced banana
- 250ml soya milk
- 1 tsp honey
- a little grated nutmeg
- 2 tsp chopped hazelnuts , to serve

Method

STEP 1

Blend the banana with soya milk, honey and a little grated nutmeg until smooth. Pour into two large glasses and top with the toasted, chopped hazelnuts to serve.

Dried fruit energy nuggets

Prep:10 mins

Makes 6

Ingredients

- 50g soft dried apricot
- 100g soft dried date
- 50g dried cherry
- 2 tsp coconut oil
- 1 tbsp toasted sesame seed

Method

STEP 1

Whizz apricots with dates and cherries in a food processor until very finely chopped. Tip into a bowl and use your hands to work in coconut oil. Shape the mix into walnut-sized balls, then roll in sesame seeds. Store in an airtight container until you need a quick energy fix.

Carrot hummus with pitta dippers

Prep:15 mins

Makes enough for 4

Ingredients

- 1 large carrot , peeled, cut into chunks and boiled until very tender
- 1 tub hummus
- 1 lemon , halved
- small bunch coriander (optional)
- 2 pitta breads or 4 small ones, toasted and sliced

Method

STEP 1

Grate the cooked carrot – don't worry if it turns to mush, this is what you want.

STEP 2

Tip the hummus into a bowl, add the carrot and mix well.

STEP 3

Add a squeeze of lemon juice, but mind you don't squirt it in your eyes.

STEP 4

Snip the coriander into little pieces using scissors and stir it into the hummus. Serve with the toasted pitta bread.

Pitta pockets

Prep:5 mins

Serves 1

Ingredients

1 wholemeal pitta bread

3 tbsp hummus

2 handfuls watercress, spinach and rocket salad mix

1 tsp olive oil

Method

STEP 1

Halve the pitta bread into 2 pockets and toast until opened. Slather the inside of each with hummus. Stuff with salad, drizzle with olive oil and tuck in.

Apple & sultana muffins

Prep:15 mins **Cook:**25 mins

Makes 12

Ingredients

- 200g self-raising flour
- 1 tsp baking powder
- 1 tsp cinnamon
- 50g wholemeal flour

- 100g golden caster sugar
- 2 eggs
- 125ml semi-skimmed milk
- 4 tbsp sunflower oil
- 2 apples , grated
- 100g sultana

Method

STEP 1

Heat oven to 180C/160C fan/gas 4. In a large bowl mix the self-raising flour, baking powder, cinnamon, wholemeal flour and golden caster sugar.

STEP 2

In another bowl, mix the eggs, semi-skimmed milk and sunflower oil. Pour the wet ingredients into the dry and mix well, then stir in the grated apples and sultanas.

STEP 3

Divide the mix between 12 muffin cases and bake for 25 mins. Cool on a wire rack, then pack in a container for lunch.

Cooking with kids: Chocolate cornflake cakes

Prep:10 mins **Cook:**5 mins

Makes 12

Ingredients

- 50g butter
- 100g milk or dark chocolate, broken into chunks
- 3 tbsp golden syrup
- 100g cornflakes

Method

STEP 1

Children: Weigh out the ingredients. Older children can do this by themselves with supervision and little ones can help to pour or spoon ingredients into the weighing scales. Put 50g butter, 100g milk or dark chocolate, broken into chunks and 3 tbsp golden syrup in a saucepan or microwavable bowl. Put 100g cornflakes in another large bowl.

STEP 2

Grown ups: Melt the weighed butter, chocolate and golden syrup in the saucepan over a low heat or briefly in the microwave. Allow to cool a little before pouring over the cornflakes.

STEP 3

Children: Stir the ingredients together gently using a wooden spoon. Spoon the mixture into 12 cupcake cases arranged on a muffin tray (or baking sheet, if you don't have one). Grown ups will need to do this for younger children or simply arrange on a tray and let the mess happen. Put in the fridge to set.

Cooking with kids: Spaghetti & meatballs with hidden veg sauce

Prep:15 mins **Cook:**30 mins

Serves 6 (4 children, 2 adults)

Ingredients

For the meatballs

- 300g good quality pork sausage (about 4 large or 8 chipolatas)
- 500g lean beef mince
- 1 small onion , coarsely grated
- 1 carrot , finely grated
- 1 tbsp dried oregano
- 50g parmesan , finely grated, plus extra to serve
- 1 medium egg
- 1 tbsp olive oil

For the tomato sauce

- 1 tbsp olive oil
- 1 courgette , coarsely grated
- 3 garlic cloves , finely grated
- 1 tbsp tomato purée
- pinch caster sugar
- splash red wine vinegar
- 2x tins chopped tomato

To serve

- cooked spaghetti

Method

STEP 1

Children: Squeeze all the sausage meat out of the sausage skins into a large bowl and add the mince. Tip all the rest of the meatball ingredients, except the olive oil, into the bowl and season with black pepper then squish everything together through your hands until completely mixed. Keep an eye on younger children to make sure they don't taste any of the raw mix.

STEP 2

Children: Roll the meatball mix into walnut-sized balls and place them on a plate – this is a job children as young as 2 can help with and a great job to help teach older children basic division.

STEP 3

Grown ups: While the children are rolling the meatballs make the sauce. Heat the oil in a large saucepan. Add the courgette and garlic and cook for 5 mins until soft and mushy. Stir in the tomato puree, sugar and vinegar leave for 1 min then tip in the tomatoes and simmer for 5 mins. If your children like courgettes then you can leave the sauce chunky. But if, like mine, they hate courgettes then blitz the sauce with a hand blender – either way continue to simmer sauce gently while you cook the meatballs. If your child is confident with heat, from 7+ they can cook the sauce with supervision.

STEP 4

Grown ups: Heat the oil in a large frying pan and, working in batches, brown the meatballs on all sides then pop them into the sauce – continue to simmer the sauce for 15 mins, stirring very gently until the meatballs are cooked through. Serve with cooked spaghetti, extra grated Parmesan and a few torn basil leaves your child has picked and torn.

Cooking with kids: Fajitas

Prep: 25 mins **Cook:** 10 mins

Serves a family of 3-5 depending on ages

Ingredients

- 4 chicken breasts , cut into chunks
- olive oil , for frying

For the marinade

- 4 limes , juice only
- 2 tsp fajita seasoning
- 4 spring onions , finely sliced

- 1 fat garlic clove , crushed

For the salsa

- 1 red pepper
- ½ jar roasted pepper (we used Gaea Red Peppers Flame Roasted 290g)
- 1 small apple , peeled
- 4 ripe tomatoes
- ½ lime , juice only
- small bunch coriander , leaves picked
- chilli sauce , to taste (optional)

For the guacamole

- 2 very ripe avocados , halved and stone removed
- ½ lime , juice only
- grated cheese , to serve

To serve

- 6 - 8 tortillas (you can now get mini tortillas for kids)
- soured cream (optional)

Method

STEP 1

Grown-ups: Put the chicken and marinade ingredients in a bowl and cover. Put in the fridge for at least two hours.

STEP 2

Children: If your children are 5 or over, you can get them to roughly chop the pepper, roasted pepper, apple and tomatoes for the salsa using a good quality firm plastic knife or cutlery knife. Otherwise do this yourself. Younger children can pick the leaves from the coriander and mix them into the salsa.

STEP 3

Grown-ups: Tip the salsa ingredients into a food processor, along with the lime juice and a little seasoning and pulse until finely chopped. Take out 2 large spoons of the mixture for younger children, then add chilli sauce, if using, and pulse again to combine.

STEP 4

Children: Squeeze or spoon the avocado into a bowl and use a potato masher to mash it. Stir in the lime juice and some black pepper with a spoon. Lime juice can sting so grown ups may want to squeeze them for younger children.

STEP 5

Grown-ups: Heat a little olive oil in a frying pan and pour the contents of the chicken bowl into the pan. Cook for 5- 8 minutes or until the chicken chunks are cooked through.

STEP 6

Children: Put the grated cheese, salsa (for grown-ups and children), guacamole and sour cream in separate colourful bowls to put on the table.

STEP 7

Grown-ups: Heat the tortillas according to the pack instructions and put the cooked chicken in a bowl. Show children how to fill and roll their tortilla.

STEP 8

Children: Lay out your tortilla, choose your toppings, roll them up and eat!

Cooking with kids: Chunky fish fingers

Prep:15 mins **Cook:**15 mins

Serves 2 adults and 2-3 kids

Ingredients

- 500g skinless, boneless chunky white fish fillet (we used haddock), cut into neat thumb-sized strips
- 100g plain flour , seasoned
- 3 large eggs , beaten
- 200g dried breadcrumb
- large pinch turmeric (optional)
- vegetable oil , for frying

Method

STEP 1

Grown ups and children: Get 3 shallow dishes and set up a production line of flour then egg then breadcrumbs. Children can pour the ingredients into each dish and crack and beat the eggs. If you want the breadcrumbs to be golden then mix through the turmeric. Place a large empty plate at the end of the line to put the uncooked fish fingers on.

STEP 2

Children: Show children how to methodically dip a finger of fish in the flour, shaking off any excess, then dredge it through the egg and finally roll it in the breadcrumbs so it's completely coated and place it on the plate. This is a job kids as young as 2 can help with but it's a messy one so they may need a wipe down halfway through. The fish fingers can now be laid on a tray and frozen then placed into a bag.

STEP 3

Grown ups: To cook the fingers heat the oil in a frying pan and cook the fingers for 3-4 mins on each side. Place on a tray lined with kitchen paper and keep warm in a low oven, if cooking in batches. Alternatively, preheat the oven to 200C/180C fan/ gas mark 6. Brush a tray with a little oil, cook the fish fingers for about 10 - 12 mins until golden and cooked through, turn over half way through cooking time.

Chocolate muffins

Prep:10 mins **Cook:**25 mins

Serves 6

Ingredients

- 125g plain flour
- 25g cocoa powder
- 1 tsp baking powder
- 1 large egg
- 60g caster sugar
- 2 tbsp vegetable oil
- 100ml whole milk
- 50g chocolate chips (optional)
- 100g icing sugar

Method

STEP 1

Heat the oven to 180C/160C fan/gas 4. Line a muffin tin with six muffin cases. Sieve the flour, cocoa and baking powder into a medium bowl. Mix together the egg, sugar, oil and milk together in a jug, then gradually pour into the dry ingredients (add chocolate chips now to make double chocolate muffins, if you like) and mix until combined.

STEP 2

Spoon the mixture evenly into the cake cases and bake for 20-25 mins until a skewer inserted into the middle comes out clean. Remove from the oven and leave to cool.

STEP 3

Meanwhile, gradually mix ½-1 tbsp water into the icing sugar until you have a loose consistency that's not too runny. Drizzle the icing over the muffins once cool.

Honey & spice cookies

Prep:30 mins **Cook:**12 mins

Makes approx 35

Ingredients

- 400g plain flour
- 200g butter
- 1 beaten egg
- 2 tbsp festive spice
- 100g golden caster sugar
- 2 tbsp honey
- ½ tsp cream of tartar
- melted dark chocolate

Method

STEP 1

Rub the butter into the flour in a large bowl until you have fine crumbs. Stir in the beaten egg, our festive spice, golden caster sugar, honey and cream of tartar. Stir unil a soft dough forms, then wrap in cling film and chill for 20-30 mins.

STEP 2

Heat oven to 180C/160C fan/gas 4. Roll out the dough, cut into festive shapes and bake for 10-12 mins on lined baking trays. Dip in melted dark chocolate, if you like.

Chicken & sweetcorn ramen

Prep:5 mins **Cook:**10 mins

Serves 2

Ingredients

- 1 pack instant ramen noodles
- 600ml chicken stock
- ½ cooked chicken breast , sliced
- 4 tbsp sweetcorn , peas or chopped beans

- 1 egg
- sesame oil , to serve (optional)

Method

STEP 1

Put the noodles in a pan (don't add the flavour sachet). Pour over the stock, bring to the boil, then simmer until cooked (follow pack instructions for cooking time).

STEP 2

Lift the noodles out of the pan and transfer to two bowls. Bring the stock in the pan back to a simmer, then add the chicken and cook until heated through. Scoop the chicken out with a slotted spoon, then transfer to the bowls. Warm the sweetcorn or cook the peas or beans in the stock, bringing back to the boil if you need to, then transfer to the bowl.

STEP 3

Meanwhile, cook the egg in a pan of boiling water for 6 mins. Remove carefully and cool under the cold tap, then peel and halve. Add an egg half to each bowl, then bring the stock back to a simmer and pour it over the noodles. Add a few drops of sesame oil, if you like.

Ghoulish Halloween cupcakes

Prep:1 hr **Cook:**25 mins

Serves 12

Ingredients

- 100g butter , cubed
- 100g plain chocolate
- 100g golden caster sugar
- 1 egg
- ½ tsp vanilla extract
- 125g self-raising flour
- 250g white fondant icing
- 500g mixed pack coloured fondant

You will need

- paper cases
- icing pens
- icing eyes

Method

STEP 1

Heat oven to 160C/140C fan/gas 3. Line a 12-hole cupcake tin with paper cases. Gently melt the butter, chocolate, sugar and 100ml hot water together in a large saucepan, stirring occasionally. Set aside to cool a little.

STEP 2

Stir the egg and vanilla into the chocolate mixture. Put the flour in a large mixing bowl, then add the chocolate mixture and stir until smooth. Divide the mixture evenly between the paper cases; they should be about three-quarters full. Bake on a low shelf in the oven for 20-22 mins. Press on the cupcakes to check if they're cooked; the tops should spring back. Remove from the oven and leave to cool.

STEP 3

Use the image above as a guide to decorating the cupcakes. Packet fondant can often be quite sticky; if yours is, pat walnut-sized lumps of fondant over the surface of each cake, rather than trying to roll it all out. Knead yellow and red fondant together to make orange icing. Make extra decorations, like hair and mouths, out of fondant and stick them on using a little water. Use the icing pens to draw lines in the fondant. Add icing eyes wherever you like.

Cheese & chorizo or prosciutto skewers

Prep:20 mins **Cook:**5 mins

Serves 6

Ingredients

- 150g manchego
- 12 slices chorizo
- 6 red grapes , halved
- 12 mini mozzarella balls
- 12 small basil leaves (optional)
- 6 slices prosciutto , halved

Method

STEP 1

Heat oven to 180C/160C fan/gas 4. Cut the manchego into 12 cubes or oblongs. Fold a slice of chorizo around each piece of cheese and push a cocktail stick through the middle to secure it. Push half a grape on to one side, then transfer skewers to a baking tray and cook for 5 mins. Cool.

STEP 2

Wrap each mozzarella ball in basil, top with half a slice of prosciutto and push a skewer through. To serve young children, slide everything off the skewers.

Super-versatile meatballs

Prep:15 mins **Cook:**30 mins

Serves 4

Ingredients

- ½ medium onion , roughly chopped
- 85g fresh white breadcrumbs
- 1 tbsp chopped parsley
- 200g lean pork mince
- 200g turkey mince
- grating of nutmeg
- 1 tbsp plain flour plus more for dusting
- rapeseed oil for frying
- 1 tbsp butter
- 400ml hot beef stock
- 2 tbsp single cream

Method

STEP 1

Whizz the onion, breadcrumbs and parsley in a food processor until finely chopped. Add the mince, nutmeg and seasoning. Use the pulse button to mix but don't overdo it or you'll make a paste. Form into 20 walnut-sized meatballs and dust with flour.

STEP 2

Heat the oil in a large frying pan and fry the meatballs in batches until they are browned all over, then carefully lift them out with a slotted spoon and drain them on kitchen paper.

STEP 3

Melt the butter in the pan, then sprinkle over the flour and stir well. Cook for 2 mins, then slowly whisk in the stock. Keep whisking until it is a thick gravy, then return the meatballs to the pan and cook them for 5 mins. Stir in the cream. Before serving, check one to see if they are cooked all the way through to the centre.

BBQ sausages with smoky tomato sauce

Prep:5 mins **Cook:**30 mins

Serves 6

Ingredients

- 24 chipolata sausages

For the smoky tomato sauce

- 100g low-sugar ketchup
- 100g passata
- 100ml cider vinegar
- 100g light brown soft sugar
- 1 garlic clove , crushed
- 1 tsp chipotle paste
- 2 tbsp butter

You will need

- 8 wooden or metal skewers (if using wooden, soak in water for at least 15 mins first)

Method

STEP 1

To make the sauce, combine the ingredients in a saucepan, then season. Bring to the boil and bubble for 3-4 mins until the sugar has completely dissolved and the sauce is glossy. Leave to cool. The sauce will keep in the fridge for up to two weeks or freeze for up to two months.

STEP 2

Heat a barbecue until the coals are glowing white hot. Lay six of the sausages next to each other and push one stick through one end of all the sausages and the other stick through the other ends so the sausages look like a ladder (leave a gap between each sausage). Repeat with the other sausages in batches of six.

STEP 3

Barbecue the sausages on each side until they are browned and cooked through, then brush with sauce and cook for a minute on each side until sticky-looking. Brush once more with the sauce before serving, and serve the rest of the sauce on the side.

Polar bear peppermint creams

Prep:30 mins

makes 15-20

Ingredients

- 250g icing sugar
- 1 egg white , beaten
- few drops of peppermint essence
- 15 chocolate sweets (we used Waitrose blue and green chocolate beans)

Method

STEP 1

Sieve the icing sugar into a large bowl. Mix in the egg white, a little at a time – stop adding it when you have a soft dough that feels like plasticine.

STEP 2

Add 3 drops of the peppermint essence, mix well and taste. Add another drop if it isn't minty enough.

STEP 3

Roll half the mixture into 15 balls, about the size of cherry tomatoes, then flatten them with your hand to make the bear heads.

STEP 4

Place on sheets of baking parchment on a large board or tray. Using half the remaining mixture, make blueberry-sized balls and flatten them out onto the heads to make snouts. Add chocolate sweets for the noses.

STEP 5

Use the rest of the mixture to make the ears. Shape them into tiny balls and press them gently into the top of the heads with your fingertips. Use a cocktail stick to shape the eyes.

STEP 6

Leave the polar bears to dry for 3-4 hrs, or overnight. Eat within 1 month.

Unbelievably easy mince pies

Prep:30 mins - 40 mins **Cook:**20 mins

Makes 18 pies

Ingredients

- 225g cold butter, diced
- 350g plain flour
- 100g golden caster sugar
- 280g mincemeat
- 1 small egg, beaten
- icing sugar, to dust

Method

STEP 1

To make the pastry, rub the butter into the flour, then mix in the golden caster sugar and a pinch of salt.

STEP 2

Combine the pastry into a ball – don't add liquid – and knead it briefly. The dough will be fairly firm, like shortbread dough. You can use the dough immediately, or chill for later.

STEP 3

Heat the oven to 200C/180C fan/gas 6. Line 18 holes of two 12-hole patty tins, by pressing small walnut-sized balls of pastry into each hole.

STEP 4

Spoon the mincemeat into the pies. Take slightly smaller balls of pastry than before and pat them out between your hands to make round lids, big enough to cover the pies.

STEP 5

Top the pies with their lids, pressing the edges gently together to seal – you don't need to seal them with milk or egg as they will stick on their own. *Will keep frozen for up to one month.*

STEP 6

Brush the tops of the pies with the beaten egg. Bake for 20 mins until golden. Leave to cool in the tin for 5 mins, then remove to a wire rack. To serve, lightly dust with the icing sugar. *Will keep for three to four days in an airtight container.*

Weaning recipe: Chicken meatballs

Prep:15 mins **Cook:**10 mins

serves family of 4 (makes 16-20 meatballs)

Ingredients

- ½ celery stick , cut into small chunks
- 1 small carrot , cut into small chunks
- 500g boneless skinless chicken thighs, cut into chunks
- a few chives , snipped
- oil , for greasing

To serve

- boiled rice
- steamed broccoli

Method

STEP 1

Heat oven to 200C/180C fan/gas 6. Blitz the celery, carrot, chicken and chives in a food processor until finely chopped. You may need to use a spatula to scrape the sides of the bowl a few times.

STEP 2

Shape into small meatballs. *If freezing, space out on a tray and put in the freezer. Once frozen, transfer to a freezer bag and take them out when needed. Defrost thoroughly in the fridge before cooking.*

STEP 3

To cook, put on a baking tray lined with greased foil and bake for 10 mins or until browned and cooked through.

STEP 4

Served with boiled rice and steamed broccoli.

Smoky black bean chilli

Prep:15 mins **Cook:**2 hrs and 55 mins

Serves 4

Ingredients

- 1-2 tsp chipotle paste
- 400g black beans or kidney beans, drained
- small bunch coriander , chopped
- 4 (or more) tortilla bowls (we used Old El Paso Stand 'n' Stuff)
- 1 avocado , sliced

- 1 lime , juiced
- soured cream , to serve
- grated cheddar , to serve

For the mince base

- 1 tbsp olive oil
- 1 small onion , finely chopped
- 1 garlic clove , crushed
- ½ celery stick, finely sliced
- 1 small carrot , finely chopped
- 500g beef mince , 10% fat
- 3 tbsp tomato & vegetable purée
- 200ml passata
- 50ml milk

Method

STEP 1

Heat half of the oil in a pan, add the onion and fry until it starts to soften, then add the garlic, celery and carrot and cook until soft. Meanwhile, heat the remaining oil in a separate frying pan and fry the mince in batches, scooping each batch out with a slotted spoon and leave any excess oil behind.

STEP 2

Add the mince to the veg, then stir in the tomato purée and cook for 1 min. Stir in the passata and bring to a simmer. Cover and cook over a very low heat for 1½-2 hrs, then add the milk and cook for 30 mins. If you're making the base ahead of time, you can leave it to cool at this stage then freeze for up to a month. (Defrost fully before using in the next step.)

STEP 3

Put the mince base in a pan and add 1 tsp chipotle paste, bring to a simmer and taste it – add the other tsp if you need to. Stir in the black beans and cook for 5 mins, then stir in the coriander.

STEP 4

Warm the tortilla bowls in a low oven. Serve the bowls filled with chilli and add the avocado, a squeeze of lime, soured cream and cheese.

Layered rainbow salad pots

Prep:25 mins **Cook:**12 mins

Serves 4

Ingredients

- 350g pasta shapes (De Cecco is a good brand that stays nice and firm)
- 200g green beans , trimmed and chopped into short lengths
- 160g can tuna in olive oil, drained
- 4 tbsp mayonnaise
- 4 tbsp natural yogurt
- ½ small pack chives , snipped (optional)
- 200g cherry tomatoes , quartered
- 1 orange pepper , cut into little cubes 195g can sweetcorn, drained

Method

STEP 1

Cook the pasta until it is still a little al dente (2 mins less than the pack instructions) and drain well. Cook the green beans in simmering water for 2 mins, then rinse in cold water and drain well. Mix the tuna with the mayonnaise and yogurt. Add the chives, if using.

STEP 2

Tip the pasta into a large glass bowl or four small ones, or four wide-necked jars (useful for taking on picnics). Spoon the tuna dressing over the top of the pasta. Add a layer of green beans, followed by a layer of cherry tomatoes, then the pepper and sweetcorn. Cover and chill until you're ready to eat.

Mince & pea pies

Prep:20 mins **Cook:**55 mins

Serves 4

Ingredients

- 500g lean minced beef
- 1 tbsp olive oil
- 1 onion , finely chopped
- 2 large carrots (about 200g), finely chopped
- 2 celery sticks (about 200g), finely chopped
- 1 tbsp tomato purée
- 1 beef stock cube
- 200g frozen peas

- 1 egg , lightly beaten
- 375g ready-rolled shortcrust pastry
- Tenderstem broccoli or other greens, to serve

Method

STEP 1

Fry the mince in a little oil over a high heat, stirring to break up any lumps, until it's well browned all over. Transfer the mince to a plate, then fry the onion, carrots and celery in the rest of the oil over a low heat until softened. Stir in the tomato purée and crumble in the stock cube, then return the mince to the pan and give everything a good stir. Fry for a minute, then add 300ml water. Cover with a lid and simmer for 20 mins, then remove the lid and simmer until the sauce has thickened slightly. Stir in the peas, then turn off the heat and leave to cool for 10 mins

STEP 2

Heat oven to 200C/180C fan/gas 6. Divide the mince mixture between four individual pie dishes (or use one large dish). Brush the dish rims with egg. Unroll the pastry and cut it into four pieces for the individual pies – roll the pieces out a little more to fit the pie dishes if you need to. Top each pie with some pastry, press down against the rim and trim any excess. Seal the edges with a fork, or crimp if you like, then brush the pastry with egg.

STEP 3

Poke a little hole in the top, decorate with any offcuts if you like (brushed with a little egg), then cook for 25-30 mins or until the pastry is golden and risen. Cool for 5-10 minutes before serving.

Caramelised honey carrots

Cook:35 mins

Serves 4

Ingredients

- 500g pack Chantenay carrots , trimmed
- 1 tbsp honey
- 2 tsp butter
- 1 tsp thyme leaves

Method

STEP 1

Put the carrots in a large frying pan with a lid. Cover with cold water, put the lid on and bring to a boil.

Once boiling, take the lid off and cook over a medium heat for about 25-30 mins until all the water has evaporated.

STEP 2

Reduce the heat, add the honey, butter and thyme leaves and gently cook for about 5 mins until the carrots are caramelised and golden.

Pick & mix omelette with crunchy croutons

Prep:5 mins **Cook:**5 mins

Serves 1

Ingredients

- 1 thick slice bread , cut into small cubes
- 1 tbsp olive oil
- 2 eggs
- 2 tbsp grated cheese
- your choice of 1 slice ham , 1 slice chicken, 2 slices salami, 2 slices chorizo, or a handful prawns
- your choice of a handful quartered cherry tomatoes , 2 tbsp drained sweetcorn, 2 tbsp defrosted frozen peas, or a handful rocket
- salad , to serve

Method

STEP 1

Heat ½ tbsp oil in a small non-stick frying pan. Add the bread, toss it around and fry over a medium heat until it starts to brown and crisp all over. Tip the croutons onto a plate, then carefully wipe out the pan. Shred the meat you have chosen to use or roughly chop the prawns.

STEP 2

Beat the eggs lightly with a fork and season if you want. Heat ½ tbsp oil in the frying pan, then pour in the egg. Tip the pan from side to side until the base is covered and starting to set. Add the meat and veg to the side of the omelette nearest you. Cover the pan with a lid for a minute, then add the cheese and cover for another minute. Finally add the croutons and flip the far side of the omelette towards you so that it covers the filling. Slide onto a plate and serve with whatever kind of salad you can get away with.

Homemade cocoa pops

Prep:10 mins **Cook:**16 mins

Serves 20

Ingredients

- 100g coconut oil
- 200g honey
- 100g cocoa powder
- 850g buckwheat
- 150g pack cacao nibs (if you're cooking with kids, you can substitute with chopped dark chocolate)

Method

STEP 1

Heat oven to 180C/160C fan/gas 4. Line two large baking trays with baking parchment. In a large microwaveable bowl, melt the coconut oil with the honey, cocoa powder and a pinch of sea salt. Stir in the buckwheat, covering well in the chocolate mixture.

STEP 2

Spread the mixture onto the baking trays and bake for 15 mins, stirring halfway, then mix in the cacao nibs. Allow to cool before storing in a Kilner jar or airtight container. *Best eaten within 1 month.*

Child-friendly Thai chicken noodles

Prep:10 mins **Cook:**15 mins - 20 mins

Serves 2 adults + 2 children

Ingredients

- 100g sugar snap peas
- 1 tbsp oil
- 2 spring onions , finely chopped
- 2 garlic cloves , crushed
- 1 tsp grated ginger
- 3 x chicken breasts, cut into chunks
- ½ tbsp Thai curry paste (we used Thai Taste)
- 400ml can coconut milk
- limes , juice of one, other quartered
- 50g frozen peas
- nests egg noodles
- handful chopped coriander , to serve

Method

STEP 1

Blanch the sugar snap peas in a bowl of boiling water for 2 mins, then drain. Heat the oil in a large frying pan. Add the spring onions, garlic, ginger and chicken. Gently fry for 2-3 mins. Stir in the curry paste and cook for 1 minute more. Add the coconut milk to the pan, along with a splash of water, the lime juice, peas and sugar snap peas. Gently bubble for around 5 mins until the chicken is cooked through.

STEP 2

Meanwhile, cook the noodles according to the pack instructions. Drain. Stir the noodles through the sauce, scatter with coriander and serve with a wedge of lime for squeezing over.

Caramel & coffee ice cream sandwich

Prep: 5 mins

Serves 2

Ingredients

- 1 tbsp chocolate-coated coffee beans , roughly chopped
- 2 scoops coffee ice cream , softened
- 4 caramel wafers

Method

STEP 1

Mix the chocolate coffee beans into the softened ice cream until combined, then transfer to a small loaf tin and freeze for a few hours or until solid.

STEP 2

Use cookie cutters to cut the ice cream to the same size as the waffles, then sandwich between two waffles.

Creamy salmon, prawn & almond curry

Prep: 15 mins **Cook:** 25 mins

Serves 3 (or 2 adults and 2 children)

Ingredients

- 2 tbsp oil

- 1 onion , chopped
- 2 garlic cloves , crushed
- 2 red peppers , sliced
- ½ tsp ground turmeric
- 2 tsp ground cumin
- 2 tsp ground coriander
- 1 tbsp tomato purée
- 70g ground almonds
- 1 low-salt vegetable or chicken stock cube
- 1½ tbsp double cream
- 300g green beans
- 2 salmon fillets (around 300g-350g), skin removed and cut into chunks
- 150g raw king prawns
- handful of coriander , leaves picked
- 150g brown rice , cooked, to serve
- ½ lime , cut into wedges to serve

Method

STEP 1

Heat the oil in a pan and cook the onion for 8-10 mins until starting to soften, then stir in the garlic and cook for 1 min. Add the peppers, spices, tomato purée and a splash of water. Cook for 1-2 mins until the peppers soften.

STEP 2

Add the almonds, stock cube and 500ml water to the pan, season and simmer for 10 mins. Stir in the cream. Cook the beans in a small pan of boiling water for 2 mins until just tender, then drain.

STEP 3

When you're ready to eat, add the salmon to the sauce, simmer gently for 2-3 mins until the fish turns opaque, then add the prawns and cook for a further 1 min until they turn pink. Check the salmon is cooked through (it should easily flake when gently pressed with a knife). Remove from the heat and add a little lime juice. Serve scattered with the coriander, the beans with the rice and the lime wedges for squeezing over.

Watermelon doughnuts

Prep:20 mins **Cook:**10 mins

Makes 12 large doughnuts

Ingredients

For the batter

- 200g plain flour
- 180g golden caster sugar
- 2 tsp baking powder
- ½ tsp ground cinnamon
- 250g buttermilk
- 2 medium eggs , lightly beaten
- 30g butter , melted
- 1 tsp vanilla extract

To decorate

- 300g pink candy melts
- 200g green candy melts
- 2 tbsp vegetable oil
- 30g dark chocolate chips

You will need

- 12-hole doughnut tin

Method

STEP 1

Heat oven to 220C/200C fan/gas 7. Put all the dry ingredients together in a bowl and mix well with a whisk to distribute the cinnamon and baking powder. Add the wet ingredients and mix until just combined. Pour the batter into a piping bag and fill the doughnut pan until each hole is approximately three quarters full. Do this in batches if needed.

STEP 2

Bake for 9–10 minutes until risen, golden brown and the tops are springy to the touch. Allow to cool for a couple of mins then turn out onto a wire rack to cool completely. If the doughnuts have lost their holes during baking use a small cutter or piping nozzle to recut them.

STEP 3

Put your pink candy melts in a microwaveable bowl with 1 tbsp vegetable oil. Melt at 30 second intervals at a medium heat until silky and completely melted. Spoon the pink candy melt over the top of each doughnut wiping off any drips that fall down the edge. Leave on a wire rack until set (about 5-10 mins). Do not throw away the excess pink!

STEP 4

Meanwhile melt the green candy melts in the same way. Hold your doughnuts on the edge and roll them through the green candy melts only covering the outside not the pink. Leave to set.

STEP 5

Cut the chocolate chips in half to create watermelon seed shapes. Dip a cocktail stick into the pink candy melt and mark out the spots to place your seeds then stick on the chocolate chips.

Pea & pesto soup with fish finger croûtons

Prep:5 mins **Cook:**15 mins

Serves 4

Ingredients

- 500g frozen pea
- 4 medium potatoes, peeled and cut into cubes
- 1l hot vegetable stock
- 300g pack fish finger (about 10)
- 3 tbsp green pesto

Method

STEP 1

Tip the peas and potatoes into a large saucepan, then pour in the stock. Bring to the boil and simmer for 10 mins, until the potato chunks are tender. Meanwhile, grill the fish fingers as per pack instructions until cooked through and golden. Cut into bitesize cubes and keep warm.

STEP 2

Take a third of the peas and potatoes out of the pan with a slotted spoon and set aside. Blend the rest of the soup until smooth, then stir in the pesto with the reserved vegetables. Heat through and serve in warm bowls with the fish finger croûtons on top.

Cherry ripple, chocolate & rose ice cream

Prep:15 mins

Plus 4 hrs freezing

Serves 8

Ingredients

- 425g can pitted cherries in syrup, drained (reserve the syrup)
- ½ tsp rose water
- 600ml double cream
- ½a 397g can condensed milk
- 100g bar of dark chocolate , chopped (you want a nice mixture of chunks and smaller bits)
- shortbread biscuits , cones and extra cherries, to serve (optional)

Method

STEP 1

 Line a 900g loaf tin with parchment or cling film. Tip the cherries into a food processor with 2 tbsp syrup from the tin, add the rose water and blend to a purée.

STEP 2

Whip the cream until it holds soft peaks, then stir in the condensed milk and half the cherry purée. Pour roughly a third of the mixture into the loaf tin, swirl through some of the purée and scatter with chocolate, then repeat the layers until you've used all the ingredients up. Freeze for at least 4 hrs. Turn out the ice cream, slice and serve with biscuits and extra cherries, or use a scoop for balls to fill ice cream cones.

Weaning recipe: Fish pie bites

Prep:20 mins **Cook:**1 hr and 45 mins

Makes 8-9 bites

Ingredients

- 1 medium baking potato
- 1 small salmon fillet , about 120g
- 1 tbsp frozen sweetcorn and peas, defrosted
- 1 tsp fresh chives , snipped into little strands
- 25g mild cheddar , grated
- ½ small egg , beaten
- oil , for greasing

Method

STEP 1

Heat the oven to 200C/ 180 fan/ gas 6. Wrap the potato in foil, place on a baking tray and roast in the oven for 1 hour 15 mins. Wrap the fish in foil, put on the same tray and continue cooking for around 10-12 mins until opaque and cooked through.

STEP 2

Once cooked, halve the potato and scoop out the filling. Flake the fish, removing any bones and discarding the skin.

STEP 3

Grease a baking tray with a little oil. Mash the potato, then mix through the flaked fish, veg, chives, cheese and egg. Allow to cool a little, then take golf-ball sized dollops of mixture and form into little croquette shapes. Arrange on a foil-lined tray and chill in the fridge for 30 mins. *If freezing, put the tray in the freezer instead. Once frozen, transfer to a freezer bag and take them out when needed. Thoroughly defrost in the fridge before cooking.*

STEP 4

To cook, heat the oven to 200C/ 180 fan/ gas 6. Arrange as many as you need on a baking tray and cook for around 15 mins or until golden and cooked through. The inside will be very hot so make sure it's sufficiently cooled before serving to your little one.

Halloween toffee apples

Prep:20 mins **Cook:**10 mins

Serves 8

Ingredients

- 8 red apples
- 400g caster sugar
- 1 tsp lemon juice
- 4 tbsp golden syrup
- red or black food colouring
- red or black food glitter (optional)

You will need

- 8 sturdy, clean twigs or lolly sticks

Method

STEP 1

Pull any stalks off the twigs and push the sharpest end of each stick (or the lolly sticks) into the stalk-end of each apple, making sure it is firmly wedged in. Put a large piece of baking parchment onto a wooden board.

STEP 2

Tip the sugar into a large saucepan and add the lemon juice and 100ml water. Bring to a simmer and cook until the sugar has dissolved. Swirl the pan gently to move the sugar around, but don't stir. Add the golden syrup and bubble the mixture (be careful it doesn't boil over) until it reaches 'hard crack' stage or 150C on a sugar thermometer. If you don't have a thermometer, test the toffee by dropping a small amount into cold water. It should harden instantly and, when removed, be brittle. If it's soft, continue to boil. When it's ready, drip in some food colouring and swirl to combine. Add the glitter, if using, and turn off the heat.

STEP 3

Working quickly, dip each apple into the toffee, tipping the pan to cover all the skin. Lift out and allow any excess to drip off before putting on the baking parchment. Repeat with the remaining apples. Gently heat the toffee again if you need to. Best eaten on the same day.

Malted milk melting snowman cake

Prep:1 hr **Cook:**1 hr and 25 mins

Serves 25 - 30

Ingredients

For the sponges

- 500g unsalted butter , softened, plus extra for greasing
- 500g golden caster sugar
- 10 eggs
- 200g plain flour
- 200g full-fat natural yogurt
- 460g self-raising flour
- 4 tbsp malt extract (or 2 tbsp vanilla paste)
- 1 tbsp full-fat milk (or 2 tbsp if using vanilla paste)

For the buttercream

- 400g unsalted butter , softened
- 700g icing sugar
- 2 tbsp malt extract (or 1 tbsp vanilla paste)
- 1 tbsp full-fat milk

For the drippy ganache

- 100g white chocolate
- ½ tsp vegetable oil

To decorate

- 30g black fondant
- 30g bright orange fondant
- 1 wooden dowel , cut the same length as the nose
- 2-3 giant chocolate buttons
- 2 white chocolate Mikado sticks , for the arms

You will need

- 2 x 20cm cake tins
- 16cm hemisphere cake tin
- 23cm cake board
- 16cm cake board

- squeezy bottle

Method

STEP 1

Heat oven to 160C/140C fan/gas 3. Grease two 20cm round cake tins and line with baking parchment. Heavily grease a 16cm hemisphere cake tin and stand on a ramekin on a baking sheet to hold it steady.

STEP 2

First, make the sponges. Using electric beaters or a tabletop mixer, beat the butter and sugar together until pale and fluffy. Pour the eggs in, one at a time, giving the mix a thorough beating before adding the next. If the mix starts to look curdled, add 2 tbsp of the plain flour. Beat in the yogurt.

STEP 3

Mix both the flours together, adding ½ tsp salt, and slowly beat into the batter, followed by the malt extract (or vanilla paste) and milk. Spoon half the mixture into one of the 20cm tins, and split the remaining half between the other 20cm tin and the 16cm hemisphere. Bake the smaller amount of cake batter in the 20cm tin and the 16cm tin for 1 hr, and the larger amount for 1 hr 20 mins or until a skewer comes out clean when inserted into the middle of the cakes. Cool in the tin for 10 mins before turning out onto a wire rack to cool completely. *Can be frozen at this stage for up to three months.*

STEP 4

Meanwhile, make the buttercream by beating all the butter and half the icing sugar together using an electric whisk or tabletop mixer. Add the rest of the icing sugar once incorporated, followed by the malt extract (or vanilla paste) and milk. Set aside until ready to use.

STEP 5

To assemble, halve the largest 20cm cake horizontally so you are left with two equal-sized sponges the same size as the remaining 20cm cake. Put a blob of buttercream onto a 23cm cake board (or cake stand) and spread using a palette knife. Stick one of the sponges to the board. Spread a thick layer of buttercream on top of the cake and sandwich another sponge on top. Spread over another thick layer and sit the final sponge on top. Using a palette knife, coat the entire cake in a thin layer of buttercream and smooth the sides and top carefully, working around the whole cake, scraping off any excess icing. Chill in the freezer for 10 mins or in the fridge for 1 hr until set.

STEP 6

Meanwhile, put the hemisphere sponge on the smaller cake board and halve horizontally. Fill the middle with some buttercream, sandwich with the top and coat the entire cake in a thin layer of buttercream. Chill in the freezer for 5 mins or in the fridge for 30 mins.

STEP 7

Take the larger cake out of the fridge/ freezer and coat in another layer of buttercream. Take care when covering this time, as you want a smooth finish to the cake. Running the palette knife under hot water helps smooth over the sides once it is coated completely. Chill again for 5 mins in the freezer.

STEP 8

Cover the hemisphere sponge with buttercream and smooth over with the palette knife. Carefully lift the hemisphere onto the centre of the cake (as the sponge has been frozen you shouldn't leave finger marks). Press down lightly to set on the buttercream. If there is a gap around the rim, use a small palette knife to fill in with any remaining buttercream. Chill for 10-15 mins.

STEP 9

Meanwhile, make the eyes and nose using coloured fondant. Roll the black fondant into two balls for the eyes, and five smaller balls for the mouth. Roll the orange fondant into a carrot shape. Leave to set and harden slightly while you make the drippy ganache.

STEP 10

Make the drippy ganache by mixing the chocolate and oil and microwaving for 30 secs, stirring and then giving it another 30 secs until melted. Transfer to a squeezy bottle, then pour down the edges of the round cake to create the melting snow effect.

STEP 11

To finish the cake, stick the eyes to the head using a little remaining buttercream. Poke the wooden dowel into the carrot nose, leaving some poking out to stick it to the face. Stick the five small black fondant balls for the mouth and the chocolate buttons down the front of the cake for buttons. Insert the Mikado sticks on either side for the arms. Bring the cake to room temperature before serving.

Chicken schnitzel with coleslaw

Prep:30 mins **Cook:**10 mins

Serves 4

Ingredients

For the schnitzel

- 4 small chicken breasts
- 3 tbsp grated parmesan
- 100g flour
- 1 large egg , beaten
- 75g dried breadcrumbs (we used panko)
- 75ml vegetable oil

For the coleslaw

- 300g white cabbage , shredded
- 1 large carrot , peeled and grated
- 6 spring onions , sliced diagonally
- 1 red-skinned apple , grated
- 150g pot natural yogurt
- juice 0.5 lemon
- 2 tsp English mustard

Method

STEP 1

For the coleslaw, get your child to mix all the ingredients in a large bowl. Season a little and set aside.

STEP 2

Place a layer of cling film on your work surface and pop the chicken fillets on top. Cover with another piece of cling film and, using a rolling pin, ask your child to bash the chicken until it is 2-3mm thick.

STEP 3

Put the flour on a plate and season, then put the egg on another plate. Get your child to dip the chicken in the flour to coat, then into the egg.

STEP 4

Mix together the breadcrumbs and Parmesan in a shallow bowl, then ask your child to toss the chicken in the mixture to completely coat in the crumbs. Put the chicken on a plate and chill in the fridge until ready to eat if you're not cooking them straight away.

STEP 5

Heat the oil in a large frying pan over a fairly high heat and cook the chicken schnitzels two at a time. Sizzle them for 2-3 mins each side until completely golden, then lift out onto kitchen paper to drain. You can keep them warm in a low oven while you cook the rest. Serve with the coleslaw.

Orange and raspberry Hey Duggee cake

Prep:1 hr and 30 mins **Cook:**1 hr and 40 mins

Serves 16

Ingredients

For the cake

- 300g unsalted butter , room temperature
- 300g caster sugar
- 2 tsp vanilla extract
- 6 large eggs
- 400g self-raising flour
- 130g natural yogurt
- 2 tbsp milk (if needed)

For the syrup

- 50g caster sugar
- 1 tsp vanilla extract

For the orange buttercream & jam filling

- 250g unsalted butter , softened
- 550g icing sugar
- 75g orange curd
- 3 tbsp raspberry jam

For the decoration

- 500g red sugarpaste
- 250g yellow sugarpaste
- 140g blue sugarpaste
- 100g brown sugarpaste

- 25g black sugarpaste
- 80cm length of yellow ribbon (optional)

Method

STEP 1

Start by making the cake. Heat oven to 180C/160C fan/gas 4 and lightly grease a 23cm deep round cake pan, lining the base with parchment paper.

STEP 2

Cream the butter and sugar together in a large bowl using an electric hand whisk until light and fluffy – this should take about 10 mins. Add the vanilla and whisk again to combine. Beat the eggs a little with a fork, and with the beaters still running, add the eggs a little bit at a time. Wait until each addition has been fully combined before adding more.

STEP 3

Once all of the eggs have been added, fold in the flour with a spatula in three additions, alternating with the yogurt. If the finished batter feels a little stiff, mix in a couple tbsp of milk to loosen it. Transfer the batter into the prepared cake pan and level out with a spatula.

STEP 4

Bake in the preheated oven for about 1 hr 30 – 1 hr 40 mins or until a skewer inserted into the middle of the cake comes out clean. If the cake is browning too quickly, cover loosely with baking parchment for the last 15 mins of cooking. Allow the cake to cool in the tin for 20 mins.

STEP 5

While the cake is cooling in the tin make the syrup. Place the sugar, 50ml water and vanilla extract into a small saucepan over a medium heat and bring to a simmer, cooking for a few mins until the sugar has dissolved. Transfer the cake onto a wire rack to cool completely then use a skewer to poke holes all over the top of the cake. Use a pastry brush to spread the syrup over the top of the cake, allowing it to soak into the sponge before adding more.

STEP 6

To make the buttercream, beat the butter and icing sugar together with an electric hand whisk until light and fluffy, then add the orange curd and whisk again to combine. If the cake is domed on the top, use a large serrated knife to level it off then cut the cake through the middle, into two layers. Place the bottom layer of cake onto a 23cm round cake board and spread a thin layer of buttercream on the cake and top with the raspberry jam. Place the second layer of cake on top and spread the remaining buttercream over the top and sides of the cake.

STEP 7

On a work surface lightly dusted with icing sugar, knead the red sugarpaste until soft and pliable. Roll it out until about 3-4mm thick and wide enough to cover the cake. Roll the sugarpaste onto the rolling pin and carefully drape over the cake. Gently smooth the sugarpaste down the sides of the cake and trim off the excess with a small sharp knife. Reserve the trimmings for the details later on.

STEP 8

Repeat the rolling process with the yellow sugarpaste but this time cutting into thin strips. Cut 30 strips approx 1.5cm x 10cm and stick to the sides of the cake all the way around, dipping your finger in water to brush onto the back of each one, which will act as glue (the strips should cover the entire height of the cake but only reach a couple of centimetres over the top of cake).

STEP 9

Next roll out the blue sugarpaste to the same thickness as the red and yellow but this time cut out a 20cm circle and stick it in place in the middle of the cake using a little water. Roll out the brown sugarpaste as well and use a thin sharp knife to cut out Duggee's face and attach to the blue circle.

STEP 10

For Duggee's clothes knead a little yellow into the remaining brown sugarpaste until it is a light brown colour and use this to cut out his shirt and lip area, sticking with a little water as before. Use the black sugarpaste to roll his eyes and nose, using your hands rather than rolling on the work surface. Use the remaining sugarpaste to shape the decorations for his outfit and mouth and stick as before with a little water. Wrap the ribbon around the bottom edge of the cake and secure with tape or a pin but remember to remove before serving. *This cake will keep in a sealed container for up to 4 days.*

Mini Egg cake

Prep: 1 hr and 15 mins **Cook:** 45 mins

Serves 16

Ingredients

- 250g butter , softened, plus a little extra, melted, for the tin
- 250g self-raising flour , plus extra for dusting
- 225g golden caster sugar
- 2 oranges , zested
- 5 large eggs
- 1 tsp baking powder

For the drizzle

- 2 oranges , juiced (use the ones you've zested)

- 2 tbsp golden caster sugar

For the icing

- 150g butter , softened
- 500g icing sugar
- 1 tsp vanilla extract
- 180g tub full-fat cream cheese

For the decoration

- 4 x 90g bags Cadbury's Mini Eggs

Method

STEP 1

Heat oven to 180C/160C fan/gas 4. Butter a bundt tin or fluted cake ring (at least 2.5-litre capacity), then dust the tin with a little flour, shaking off the excess. Beat all the cake ingredients with a pinch of salt using an electric whisk until you have a smooth batter. Spoon into the prepared tin, smoothing the top with a palette knife, then bake for 35 mins until a skewer inserted into the centre comes out mostly clean with a few dry crumbs attached.

STEP 2

For the drizzle, combine the sugar with the orange juice in a saucepan, then reduce over a medium heat to a loose syrupy consistency. Prick the base of the cake all over with a skewer, then pour over half the syrup, adding the rest once it has been absorbed, Leave the cake to cool in the tin for 15 mins, then turn out onto a wire rack to cool completely.

STEP 3

While the cake is cooling, make the icing. Beat the butter with half the icing sugar and the vanilla extract until smooth and fluffy. Add the remaining icing sugar and the cream cheese and beat again until well combined – don't overbeat or the icing will become runny.

STEP 4

Spread a thin layer of the icing over the entire cake, taking care to get into all the crevices, then pop in the fridge for 20 mins to set. If you are short of time, you can always put it in the freezer. Spread the remaining icing onto the cake in an even layer. Once iced, the cake will keep in the fridge for three days. Bring to room temperature before decorating and serving.

STEP 5

Sort the Mini Eggs into different colours (a possibly therapeutic exercise, depending on your organisational tendencies). Stick the Mini Eggs all over the top of the cake.

Lunchbox pasta salad

Prep:15 mins **Cook:**11 mins

Serves 4

Ingredients

- 400g pasta
- 4-5 tbsp fresh pesto
- 1 tbsp mayonnaise
- 2 tbsp Greek yogurt
- ½ lemon , juiced
- 200g mixed cooked veg such as peas, green beans, courgette (chop the beans and courgette into pea-sized pieces)
- 100g cherry tomatoes , quartered
- 200g cooked chicken , ham, prawns, hard-boiled egg or cheese

Method

STEP 1

Cook the pasta in boiling water until it is al dente, so about 11 mins, but refer to the pack instructions. Drain and tip into a bowl. Stir in the pesto and leave to cool.

STEP 2

When the pasta is cool, stir through the mayo, yogurt, lemon juice and veg. Spoon into lunchboxes or on to pasta plates and put the cooked chicken or protein of your choice on top. Chill until ready to eat if intended for a packed lunch.

Mozzarella & salami picnic baguette

Prep:10 mins

Plus at least 1 hr resting

Serves 4

Ingredients

- 1 white or brown baguette
- 3 tbsp fresh green pesto
- 1 beef tomato
- 1 ball mozzarella (about 200g)

- 2 handfuls baby spinach leaves
- handful basil leaves
- 6 slices salami

Method

STEP 1

Slice the baguette in half lengthways and hollow out (make crumbs from the bread centre and save for another recipe). Spread the bottom half with the pesto. Slice the tomato and layer it over the pesto. Slice the mozzarella and add in a layer over the tomato.

STEP 2

Finish with layers of spinach and basil, plus the salami, folded in half if necessary to fit the width of the baguette.

STEP 3

Wrap in baking parchment, tie with string and pop in the fridge weighted under something heavy (we used a hefty griddle pan). Leave for at least 1 hr (or overnight if you like). The flavours will mingle and the sandwich will flatten down, making it a doddle to cut up without all the ingredients falling out all over your picnic rug.

Tex-Mex meatball tacos

Prep:25 mins **Cook:**10 mins

Serves 4

Ingredients

- 400g beef mince
- 1 egg
- 35g sachet fajita spice mix
- 4 large tomatoes , roughly chopped
- small bunch coriander , roughly chopped
- 1 garlic clove , crushed
- 2 limes , 1 juiced, 1 cut into wedges to serve
- 2 tbsp olive oil
- 150ml soured cream
- 75g grated cheddar or mozzarella
- 1 avocado
- 8 taco shells

Method

STEP 1

Mix the mince with the egg, spice mix and some seasoning, then shape into 16 meatballs. Set aside in the fridge to firm up slightly while you make the sides.

STEP 2

Mix the tomatoes, coriander, ½ the garlic and ½ the lime juice in a bowl with 1 tbsp oil, season and set aside. Stir the remaining garlic into the soured cream with a handful of the grated cheese and season. Slice the avocado and squeeze over the remaining lime juice. Bring these, the taco shells and lime wedges to the table.

STEP 3

Heat the remaining oil in a large frying pan. Fry the meatballs over a medium heat for 8-10 mins until evenly browned and cooked through. Sprinkle over the remaining cheese, put a lid on the pan and cook for 1 min until melted, then let everyone help themselves.

Winter wonderland cake

Prep:1 hr **Cook:**35 mins

Serves 12

Ingredients

- 175g unsalted butter , softened, plus more for the tin
- 250g golden caster sugar
- 3 large eggs
- 225g plain flour
- 2 tsp baking powder
- 50g crème fraîche
- 100g dark chocolate , melted and cooled a little
- 3 tbsp strawberry jam
- 8-10 candy canes , red and white
- mini white meringues and jelly sweets, to decorate

For the angel frosting

- 500g white caster sugar
- 1 tsp vanilla extract
- 1 tbsp liquid glucose
- 2 egg whites

- 30g icing sugar , sifted

Method

STEP 1

Heat oven to 180C/160C fan/gas 4. Butter and line three 18cm (or two 20cm) cake tins. Beat the butter and sugar together until light and fluffy. Add the eggs, beating them in one at a time. Fold in the flour, baking powder and a pinch of salt, then fold in the crème fraîche and chocolate and 100ml boiling water.

STEP 2

Divide the cake mixture between the tins and level the tops of the batter. Bake for 25-30 mins or until a skewer inserted into the middle comes out clean. Leave to cool for 10 mins in the tin, then tip out onto a cooling rack and peel off the parchment. Set aside to cool completely.

STEP 3

To make the angel frosting, put the sugar, vanilla and liquid glucose in a pan with 125ml water. Bring to the boil and cook until the sugar has melted – the syrup turns clear and the mixture hits 130C on a sugar thermometer (be very careful with hot sugar). Take off the heat. Meanwhile, beat the egg whites until stiff then, while still beating, gradually pour in the hot sugar syrup in a steady stream. Keep beating until the mixture is fluffy and thick enough to spread – this might take a few mins as the mixture cools. Beat in the icing sugar.

STEP 4

Spread two of the sponges with jam and some of the icing mixture, then sandwich the cakes together with the plain one on top. Use a little of the frosting to ice the whole cake (don't worry about crumbs at this stage). Use the remaining icing to ice the cake again, smoothing the side, and swirling it on top. Crush four of the candy canes and sprinkle over the cake, then add the remaining whole candy canes, meringues and sweets.

Halloween biscuits

Prep:45 mins **Cook:**25 mins

Serves 7 - 8

Ingredients

For the biscuits

- 200g unsalted butter , softened
- 200g golden caster sugar
- 1 large egg

- ½ tsp vanilla extract
- 400g plain flour , plus extra for dusting
- 20g popping candy (or rainbow sprinkles for very young children)

For decoration

- White, black and grey sugar paste
- 100g icing sugar

Method

STEP 1

Heat oven to 200C/180C fan/gas 6 and line a baking sheet with baking parchment.

STEP 2

Put the butter in a bowl and beat with electric beaters until soft and creamy. Beat in the sugar, then the egg and vanilla, and finally the flour to make a dough. If the dough feels a bit sticky add a little more flour and knead it in. Wrap in cling film and put in the fridge for half an hour.

STEP 3

Heavily flour a surface and cut the pastry in half. Roll out one half to 5mm thickness. Using a cookie cutter in the shape of a ghost (or any spooky shaped cutter you like), cut out 12 ghost shapes, which will make 4 cookies. Put the cut shapes on a baking tray lined with baking paper and put back in the fridge. Repeat with the second half of the pastry. Swap into the fridge, taking the chilled ghost biscuits out.

STEP 4

Using a smaller cutter or a knife, cut a ghost-shaped hole in the middle of 4 of the biscuits on the tray, this is the space to store the surprise centre! Put these biscuits into the oven to bake for 10-12 mins, until pale but cooked through. Transfer to a wire rack to cool. Repeat with the other tray.

STEP 5

Once all the biscuits have cooled completely, they are ready to be assembled. Mix the icing sugar with 3 tbsp of water and mix well. It should be quite thick so add a little more icing sugar if the mixture is too runny. Take a biscuit without the centre missing, and spread or pipe a little icing around the edge. Press a biscuit with a centre missing on top, then sprinkle popping candy into the pocket that you have created (*or rainbow sprinkles as an alternative, if you're serving to very young children*). Spread icing on the edge of the second biscuit and press another whole biscuit on top. Set aside to firm up. Make sure you leave them for a while so they don't slide when you are finishing the decoration.

STEP 6

Once the biscuits feel firm and the icing has set, use the sugar paste to decorate them as you please, rolling it out, cutting it to shape and topping the biscuits. You may have to use a little of the icing to glue it down. Decorate with icing pens if you like.

Rice paper wraps

Prep:20 mins **Cook:**3 mins

Serves 8

Ingredients

- 50g rice vermicelli noodles
- 1 carrot , peeled
- 1 avocado , peeled and destoned
- ¼ cucumber
- 8 rice paper wraps
- 8 king prawns , peeled and cooked
- 8 mint leaves
- ½ cooked chicken breast, shredded
- sweet chilli sauce , to serve

Method

STEP 1

Put the noodles in a pan of water and bring to the boil, simmer for 3 mins, then cool under running water. Drain thoroughly.

STEP 2

Cut the carrot into matchsticks using a knife or a mandoline. Cut the avocado into strips and the cucumber into thin sticks. Soak 2 of the rice paper wraps in cold water for 1-2 mins until floppy.

STEP 3

Lift 1 sheet of rice paper out of the water, shake gently, then lay it carefully on a board. Place 2 prawns in the centre, with a mint leaf between them. Add a strip of avocado, pile some noodles on top, then add a layer of carrot and cucumber. Fold the bottom half of the rice paper over, then fold the sides in and tightly roll it up. Repeat using the second wrapper and soak 2 more to make 2 more rolls.

STEP 4

Make the rest of the rolls up using the remaining 4 wraps and the shredded chicken instead of prawns. Serve the rolls with the sweet chilli sauce for dipping.

Fluffy pancakes

Prep:10 mins **Cook:**20 mins

Makes 6

Ingredients

- 8 slices pancetta, to serve (optional)
- sunflower oil and butter, for cooking
- blueberries, to serve (optional)

For the pancakes

- 300g self-raising flour
- 1 tsp baking powder
- 1 tbsp caster sugar
- 2 medium eggs
- 1 tbsp maple syrup, plus extra to serve
- 300ml milk

Method

STEP 1

If serving with pancetta, heat oven to 200C/180C fan/gas 6. Line a baking tray with baking parchment and lay on the pancetta in a single layer. Put another piece of parchment on top, followed by a second baking tray, and bake for 12-15 mins until crisp.

STEP 2

To make the pancakes, get a little helper to weigh out and tip the flour, baking powder and sugar into a large bowl with a small pinch of salt. Crack in the eggs and whisk until smooth. Add the maple syrup and milk while whisking.

STEP 3

Heat a splash of oil and a small knob of butter in a non-stick frying pan until sizzling. Add spoonfuls of batter to make pancakes the size you like, we made 20cm pancakes for a serving size of one per person, or if you are very hungry, two per person. Cook until bubbles start to form on the surface, then flip and cook the other side. Eat straight away or keep warm in a low oven while you cook another batch. Serve pancakes with pancetta or blueberries, drizzled with extra maple syrup.

Christmas stollen with almonds & marzipan

Prep: 1 hr and 25 mins **Cook:** 1 hr and 15 mins

Plus soaking, 2-3 hrs proving, and cooling

Cuts into 10 slices

Ingredients

- 100g mixed dried fruit with peel
- 180ml apple juice
- 7g dried yeast
- 250g plain flour , plus a little extra for dusting
- 30g blanched whole almonds
- generous pinch of ground cinnamon
- generous pinch of ground aniseed or allspice
- small pinch of ground cloves
- 75g cold marzipan , cut into small pieces
- 10g butter , melted
- 1 tbsp icing sugar

Method

STEP 1

Soak the dried fruit in 100ml of hot water. Gently warm the apple juice for a few mins in a pan, then add the yeast and leave to activate for 10-15 mins (it will start to bubble).

STEP 2

Put the flour in a bowl. Stir in the yeast and apple juice mixture to form a smooth dough, then cover and leave to prove somewhere warm until roughly doubled in size, about 1-2 hrs. You can also put the dough in the fridge to rise slowly overnight.

STEP 3

Drain the fruit and add to the dough along with the nuts, spices and marzipan. Squish everything together, then turn the dough out onto a lightly floured work surface and knead until the fruit stays in the dough.

STEP 4

Shape the dough into a sausage shape and put it on a baking tray lined with baking parchment. Cover with a clean tea towel and leave to prove somewhere warm for 30 mins–1 hr until it has risen by about a quarter.

STEP 5

Heat oven to 180C/160C fan/gas 4. Bake the stollen for 20 mins, then reduce oven to 150C/130C fan/gas 2 and bake for 25-30 mins more until golden brown and firm to the touch.

STEP 6

Remove the stollen from the oven and brush all over with the melted butter. Dust with the icing sugar and leave to cool completely before slicing. Store any remaining stollen, well wrapped, in an airtight container.

Chicken satay

Prep:30 mins **Cook:**10 mins

Makes 12

Ingredients

- small piece ginger
- 2 garlic cloves
- zest and juice 1 lime
- 1 tsp clear honey
- 1 tbsp soy sauce
- 1 tbsp mild curry powder
- 3 tbsp smooth peanut butter
- 500g pack skinless chicken breast fillets
- 165ml can coconut milk
- 1 tsp vegetable oil
- cooked rice and lime wedges, to serve

For the cucumber salad

- 1 cucumber
- 2 tbsp white wine vinegar
- 1 tbsp golden caster sugar
- sweet chilli sauce (optional)
- bunch coriander leaves picked (optional)

Method

STEP 1

KIDS the writing in bold is for you. GROWN-UPS the rest is for you. **Make a yummy marinade.** Peel the ginger and help them to finely grate it and tip it into a bowl. Repeat with the garlic and lime zest. Halve the lime and get your child to juice it, then mix it in a bowl with the honey, soy, curry powder and peanut butter. Get them to give it a good mix, adding a small splash of water if it's too stiff, then help them spoon two-thirds of the mix into a small pan. Set aside for Step 4.

STEP 2

Now for some chicken bashing! Put the chicken in the sandwich bag, one breast at a time, getting your child to flatten each one with a rolling pin or a meat mallet – this isn't essential, but they like doing it.

STEP 3

Mix the chicken with the marinade you made. Cut the chicken into strips, tip it into the remaining third of the peanut-butter mix, then get your child to stir well. Cover with cling film and chill until required. *This can be done up to 3 hrs ahead.*

STEP 4

Cook your tasty sauce. While the chicken is marinating, pour the coconut milk into the pan and get your child to stir together with the peanut butter mix. The sauce needs to be heated gently and stirred – suitable for confident seven- or eight-year olds, under strict adult supervision.

STEP 5

'Sew' the chicken onto the skewers. The chicken needs to be threaded into 'S' shapes onto the skewers. Get your child to thread the skewers away from themselves, being careful of the sharp points. Younger ones might find this a little fiddly, so they could just push on small chunks.

STEP 6

Paint the tray with oil and cook the chicken. Heat the grill to high and get your child to brush a baking tray with oil. They can then line up the skewers on the tray. Grill the skewers for about 10 mins, turning occasionally, until lightly charred.

STEP 7

Make cucumber ribbons with a peeler. Using a swivel-blade peeler, get your child to peel the cucumber into a bowl, then carry on peeling the cucumber flesh into ribbons until they get to the seeds. Repeat with each side of the cucumber.

STEP 8

Mix a dressing for the cucumber. Get your child to mix the vinegar and sugar until the sugar dissolves – explain what dissolves means. Add the sweet chilli, if using, then pour over the cucumber. Add coriander if your child likes it, or serve on the side for the grown-ups. To serve, put the skewers on a platter, the sauce and salad in bowls, and serve with rice and lime wedges on the side.

Pudsey biscuits

Prep: 1 hr **Cook:** 20 mins

Makes around 20 biscuits

Ingredients

- 200g unsalted butter , softened
- 200g golden caster sugar
- 1 large egg
- ½ tsp vanilla extract
- 400g plain flour , plus extra for dusting

To decorate

- 25g icing sugar
- 50g white fondant
- coloured icing pens (writing quality)
- 25g black sugar paste
- hundreds and thousands or sweets to decorate (optional)

Method

STEP 1

Heat oven to 200C/180C fan/gas 6 and line a baking sheet with baking parchment. Put the butter in a bowl and beat it with electric beaters until soft and creamy. Beat in the sugar, then the egg and vanilla, and finally the flour to make a dough. If the dough feels a bit sticky, add a little bit more flour and knead it in.

STEP 2

Roll the dough out so it's about the thickness of a £1 coin. Cut out shapes using a Pudsey bear cutter or cut around a template you have made. Re-roll off-cuts and repeat.

STEP 3

Transfer the biscuits to the baking sheet and bake for 8-10 mins or until the edges are just brown. Leave to cool completely.

STEP 4

To decorate the biscuits: Mix the icing sugar with enough water to make a stiff paste then roll the white fondant out to 5mm thick and cut into strips to make Pudsey's eye bandage. Stick it on with the white icing. Decorate with polka dots using coloured icing pens. Make his eye, nose and mouth with the black sugar paste and add a little dot of white icing to the eye. Stick the features down with more icing. Repeat the process with most of the biscuits and decorate the rest with icing simply sprinkled with hundreds and thousands. Will keep for three days in a biscuit tin.